grow easy

Organic crops
for pots & small plots

Anna Greenland

Foreword by Raymond Blanc
Photography by Jason Ingram

MITCHELL BEAZLEY

For Hugo, with love.

'The care of the Earth is our most ancient and most worthy,
and after all our most pleasing responsibility.
To cherish what remains of it and to foster its renewal is our only hope.'

Wendell Berry, excerpt from 'The Unsettling of America'
from *The Art of the Commonplace: The Agrarian Essays.*

First published in Great Britain in 2021
by Mitchell Beazley, an imprint of
Octopus Publishing Group Ltd
Carmelite House, 50 Victoria Embankment
London EC4Y 0DZ
www.octopusbooks.co.uk

An Hachette UK Company www.hachette.co.uk

Distributed in the US by Hachette Book Group
1290 Avenue of the Americas
4th and 5th Floors, New York, NY 10104

Distributed in Canada by Canadian Manda Group
664 Annette St., Toronto, Ontario, Canada M6S 2C8

ISBN 978 1 78472 735 2

A CIP catalogue record for this book is available
from the British Library.

Printed and bound in China
10 9 8 7 6 5 4 3 2 1

Publisher: Alison Starling
Senior Managing Editor: Sybella Stephens
Copy Editor: Helen Ridge
Creative Director: Jonathan Christie
Designer: Jeremy Tilston
Illustrator: Alice Maccoll
Senior Production Controller: Emily Noto

This book is based on organic principals;
those selling produce must adhere to
Organic Standards.

Always identify wild plants correctly before
eating them. As with all herb consumption,
consult a medical herbalist if you are
pregnant, breastfeeding or have underlying
health issues. Do not give to children under
the age of two years; particular care should be
taken for children over the age of two years.

Contents

Foreword
by Raymond Blanc OBE

You and I have probably never met, yet we are united by a passion – we treasure the endless magic and miracles of a garden. Like me, you might be a gardener with a bit of experience. Or perhaps you are a novice with a compulsion to grow your own vegetables. New or old to the game, we all get excited at the thought of gardening. We like to dig, sow, plant and prune. We like to wait and watch the first seedlings coming through the soil. And, in time, we enjoy gathering the crop, so we can cook and eat it with our loved ones, or preserve it for later.

And now, through the pages of this book, you and I are about to form another connection. I have long been a great admirer of the brilliant Anna Greenland, and I know that you will become a huge fan, too.

One of the highlights of my day is an early morning stroll through the gardens at Le Manoir aux Quat'Saisons, my restaurant-hotel in Oxfordshire. It was always such a joy to see Anna there. She'd be at the potager first thing in the morning, and she'd give me a cheerful smile and a wave. Then we'd talk about vegetables and gardening and cooking and eating. Anna was the Head Vegetable Gardener at Le Manoir, and we were fully engaged on a mission to create the best gardens and grow the best vegetables. We strived only for excellence. Anna took her responsibility extremely seriously, nurturing the soil and creating astonishing beauty in every corner. Apart from being highly skilled and knowledgeable, Anna is a true artist.

It has taken a global pandemic to encourage millions of people to discover the pleasures of growing edibles. Of course, Anna is the best person to teach you the skills and help you grow your own food in a sustainable way. Local food is often the best, and what can be more local than your garden, balcony, window box or allotment? Just think – if you grow your own, you can choose varieties that are crammed with incredible flavours and amazing texture that may be unavailable in shops. You can also grow organic produce, without the need for pesticides and synthetic fertilizers. No matter how small the space, there is an unbelievable joy and many rewards that come from a connection to the soil. Every gardener or beginner knows that life is enriched by planting just a few tiny seeds or tending to a little pot of herbs.

We need people like Anna to show us how to practise this ancient art, and, in this book, she teaches the skills and shares her knowledge in a

soft, engaging voice. The Anna I know is gentle and kind, and her young soul belies sage-like wisdom and a profound understanding of the seasons. She also has a deep understanding and respect for heritage and conservation, and while she appreciates modernity, she also respects authenticity.

Grow Easy really is a superb book for those embarking on a journey to grow edibles, or for those who are more experienced and looking to hone their skills. Anna's simple recipes for preserving the harvest will help you get the most from your plot – I like to think she learned a few tricks from Le Manoir's kitchens as well as from the gardens.

Only yesterday I was looking out at my garden at home as I wrote about Anna in my own forthcoming book, *Simply Raymond*. I was writing about our exhausting trials in 2012, when Anna grew dozens of varieties of lettuce so that we could find the very best in taste, texture and appearance. Today, here I am again, looking out at my garden and once more writing about Anna, although this time for her book. I always feel privileged that Anna Greenland is a part of my life. And now I feel very happy that she is about to become a part of yours too. *Bon Appétit*!

Introduction

As I thumbed the pages of my seed catalogues in the winter of 2019, making promising lists for the season ahead, I had no idea how precious their contents were to become. Within months, the outbreak of Covid-19 had left seed companies overwhelmed with orders. Seeds have remained hot property as a new generation of growers has discovered the sheer joy of gardening.

Throughout the pandemic, the fragility of our global food system became clear, and it is local farms and our own gardens that have often provided security. Learning the basic skills to feed ourselves feels pertinent. And, practicalities aside, growing your own food feels good.

My first vegetable garden clung to the Cornish coast, battered by salty winds. All I had was a copy of *The Organic Salad Garden* by Joy Larkcom and a lot of enthusiasm. Everything was planted too close together – I didn't believe my tiny seedlings would demand so much space. I should have listened to Joy. But I was hooked – so hooked that I've made vegetable growing my life's work.

Whether you have a windowsill, balcony or small garden, this book is designed to be accessible, cutting the highbrow gardening chat. I've selected my Top 30 crops that are happy in pots and plots alike. As well as being some of the most straightforward to grow, they are also the vegetables, herbs, fruits and edible flowers that I couldn't be without.

Grow Easy enables you to start from scratch with no prior knowledge, with plant spotlights offering easy reference. And for those who would like a complete guide to their first year, I've designed a detailed crop plan for two raised beds.

It's perhaps misleading to say 'growing your own' is a walk in the park. Even the most experienced gardeners have failures, and you will need to exercise some patience. But that's the beauty of gardening. It slows you down in this frantic, modern age. You'll find beauty in the simple things, like a squash tendril clinging bravely to its trellis or a hoverfly alighting on a parsley flower.

At the root of it all is my desire to grow in a way that is in tune with the natural world. In recent times we have had to label these methods as 'organic', but we have grown without a reliance on toxic chemicals for most of our agricultural history.

Growing organically at home need not be viewed as more difficult. Making compost, planting flowers and encouraging insect friends are part of what makes gardening joyous and hardly a chore. A small space won't yield self-sufficiency but, once you've tasted your own naturally grown food, my hope is you will seek out local farms that share the same values to supplement your own produce.

Finally, there are the recipes, favourites that I roll out year on year. I like to think of you sitting amid your plants, sampling some of these – the fruits of your labour. Grow well.

Getting started

1. Hoe
2. Hori hori, or Japanese trowel (optional)
3. Spade
4. Hand trowel
5. Fork
6. Hand fork
7. Rake
8. Secateurs
9. Scissors or snips
10. Dustpan and brush
11. Knife
12. Labels
13. Watering can
14. Pencil
15. String
16. Tape measure

Tools & equipment explained

A gardener's tools should be prized, much like a chef's knives. They become worn by your hands in just the right places, and will last forever if you look after them. It's worth investing in good-quality tools that will go the distance (see Resources, pages 220–1).

← A hand trowel with a copper head is built to last.

1. HOE: For regular weeding of plants and seedlings

2. HORI HORI: For planting and weeding in place of a traditional trowel

3. SPADE: For moving soil and compost

4. HAND TROWEL: For making and planting holes and for weeding

5. FORK: For harvesting potatoes, removing sturdy plants and turning compost

6. HAND FORK: For weeding and harvesting

7. RAKE: For creating level beds for seed sowing

8. SECATEURS: For cutting plants back and general tidying

9. SCISSORS OR SNIPS: For thinning seedlings in trays and harvesting microgreens

10. DUSTPAN & BRUSH: For keeping your sowing space tidy

11. KNIFE: For harvesting leafy greens, herbs, courgettes and for general use

12. LABELS: For keeping track of varieties (opt for recyclable ones)

13. WATERING CAN: For watering small plants and seedlings (attach the rose for a gentler flow). To make your own watering bottle for windowsills, see page 69

14. PENCIL: For writing plant labels and making holes for seed sowing in module trays

15. STRING: For tying plants to supports or making straight planting lines in beds

16. TAPE MEASURE: For measuring rows and accurate plant spacings

Extras

HORTICULTURAL FLEECE, NETTING & INSECT MESH: For plant protection (see Protecting your crops, page 71)

WHEELBARROW: For moving heavy items and compost

Seed trays & pots

Seeds and plants will thrive in a range of trays and pots, from recycled food packaging to specialist gardening products. Plastic features heavily in the horticultural industry, but there are alternative options that work well (see overleaf).

If you do opt for plastic, check that it's sturdy and made to last (I've had my trays for 15 years) and/or recyclable (see Resources, pages 220–1). Or ask other gardeners or at garden centres if they have any spares you can reuse.

↑ Recycled food and drink packaging is used for raising seeds and plants.

An assortment of materials for sowing seeds.

Seed & module trays

Raising seedlings indoors in seed trays or modules gives them a head start, making them more resilient to pests and poor weather when planted outside. Either sow into trays and prick out into bigger pots (see pages 62–7) before planting, or sow into individual modules.

If you have very limited germination space, you may opt for a seed tray, as it is smaller than a module tray but can still raise many plants. But module trays are my preference and will fit on most windowsills (you will need modules to follow my raised bed crop plan on page 96).

ADVANTAGES OF MODULES

* Provide enough rooting depth for seedlings to establish well, producing robust plug plants to plant straight into beds/pots.
* Create less root disturbance and less hassle, with no pricking out needed.
* Easy to sow multiple varieties into one tray to save space.

SEED-SOWING OPTIONS

1. **Coir pellets** (peat-free). Soak in water to expand before sowing the seeds.
2. **Cardboard egg cartons** – these are shallow, so water well and pot on fast. Break off individual cells and pot on with the cardboard intact.*
3. **Module trays** – aim for a module size of around 3 × 3 × 4cm (1 × 1 × 1½in) or 4 x 4 x 4.5cm (1½ x 1½ x 1¾in). Buy trays to last. Plastic-free versions are also available (see Resources, pages 220–1). My preferred trays have between 60 and 84 individual modules.
4. **Recycled packaging** – plastic or cardboard food trays or punnets*. Always make drainage holes.
5. **Plastic seed trays** – these are long-lasting if made of sturdy plastic, but ultimately unsustainable. Seed trays made of bamboo or rice are good alternatives.
6. **The inner tube from a toilet roll*** – use for deep-rooting plants, such as beans, or cut in half to make two individual modules. Stand in seed trays.
7. **Newspaper pots*** – make your own individual modules using a paper pot maker.

Note: Seedlings dry out fast in cardboard so will need extra watering.

→ Containers for seedlings and young plants.

Pots for seedlings & young plants

Once seedlings become too big for seed trays or modules, they may need potting on (see page 66) before being planted outside. A range of pots is available for raising young plants, with various options to reduce plastic. I've kept and reused plastic pots from over the years, but also fashion my own from tin cans, yogurt pots and milk cartons.

Beans, courgettes and squashes need a good rooting depth, so should be sown straight into pots (not into seed trays or modules).

For potting on I recommend pots 9cm (3½in) in diameter and 8cm (3in) deep. These measurements won't be exact for recycled containers, but they're useful as a guide.

POT TYPES

There are a number of different pots you can use for potting on young plants.

1. **Biodegradable pots** – often made from plant fibre such as coir. Seedlings can be planted out in their pots, reducing transplant shock.
2. **Plastic pots** – reuse pots from plants bought at garden centres. Ultimately unsustainable. Bamboo and rice pots are sustainable alternatives.
3. **Terracotta** – small pots dry out fast. Keep well watered.
4. **Recycled pots** – yogurt pots, milk cartons, tin cans. These can dry out fast, so keep them well watered. Always make drainage holes in the base.
5. **Soil blocks** – these are made of compressed compost, meaning that pots aren't needed and reduces our reliance on plastic. It takes a bit of practise to make and get the soil mix and moisture levels right. Either use for starting seeds or potting on.

Compost for seed sowing & potting on

Both seed and potting composts are available to buy, and are different from homemade garden compost. Seed compost is finer than potting compost, to allow seedlings to push through without resistance. It also has fewer nutrients, as seedlings don't need them.

Potting compost is bulkier and contains the nutrients plants need for growing on. Once seedlings reach their 'true leaf' stage (when they have grown a second set of leaves after their seed leaves), it is time to pot them on. I use a multipurpose potting compost for this as well as for larger containers (see page 34 for filling larger pots).

Buying compost that is peat-free is crucial. For decades, the horticultural industry has used peat in compost mixes for its water- and nutrient-holding capacity. But lowland peat bogs, which support diverse plant and wildlife habitats as well as storing carbon, have been destroyed in the process.

What's left must be conserved.

I also buy Soil Association-approved organic compost (the Soil Association is the UK's largest organic certification body), which means it is free from synthetic fertilizers and the ingredients are suitably sourced (see Resources, pages 220–1). Although more expensive, these composts are worth it, if you wish to grow organically.

If you have the time and resources, you could try making your own:
Seed compost: 1 part garden soil (crumbly soil from molehills is perfect), 1 part leaf mould (composted leaves), 1 part horticultural sand.
Potting-on compost: 1 part garden soil, 1 part leaf mould, 1 part garden compost.

Seeds versus plants

Is it better to buy vegetable plug plants from nurseries, or to grow from seed yourself?

I encourage you to sow your own seeds, even in just a few small pots. Seeing those tiny shoots pushing through soil for the first time is an emotional, life-affirming moment. They made it! Despite chaos reigning in the wider world, your little seedlings have unfurled. It connects you wholeheartedly to the process of growing your own food, and you become devoted to their nurture.

Handling seeds will open your eyes to an endless array of beautiful forms, such as beans pretty enough for a necklace, or brittle, baby seahorse shapes that unfurl into calendula. Plus, you'll have access to a huge range of varieties otherwise unavailable. Thumbing through colourful seed catalogues is a winter delight and a promise of good things to come.

But, if you don't have any indoor space to raise seedlings or are short on time, buying ready-to-go organic plug plants is a great way to go (see Resources, pages 220–1). Starting with healthy plants is key. If buying from a garden centre, select vibrant-looking plants and avoid the leggy ones!

↑ The beautiful beans of the 'Scarlet Emperor' runner bean.
← Peat-free, organic compost gets plants off to a healthy start.

Structures for growing

→ My 8 × 6ft greenhouse is a good size for a small garden.

Raising seeds on a windowsill certainly works, but outdoor structures offer optimal light and space. Even investing in (or building) a simple cold frame is well worth it.

GREENHOUSE

An 8 × 6ft greenhouse meets my needs for a small garden (of course, if you have space, go larger because you will always fill it). My greenhouse has ground-level beds and movable benches for propagation (starting and growing on seedlings). The benches stand on the beds in the early part of the year with overwintered salads beneath. I then remove the benches in May before planting tomatoes.

Investing in a small greenhouse heater means you can start sowing certain crops as early as mid-February. With a gas or paraffin heater, it's possible for gases such as carbon monoxide and sulphur dioxide to circulate, causing harm to plants, so you need to provide ample ventilation. A temperature of 3°C (37°F) will keep the frost out, and can be raised to kick-start germination. Open the roof/side vents and doors for a spell in the morning, and keep the greenhouse vented on sunny winter days.

If you're lucky enough to have electricity outside, you could have an electric heater, which is cleaner. Heated mats are also perfect for raising seedlings; a bottom heat of around 22°C (72°F) will germinate most things.

Unheated greenhouses are still valuable spaces for raising plants in spring that won't be killed by frost. They are good halfway houses for seedlings started on a windowsill, where you can grow them on before moving them outside. Always use horticultural fleece on cold nights for extra protection.

Ensure ventilation in all spaces is good, opening doors and vents on sunny winter days. In summer, I leave my greenhouse doors and vents permanently open. To prevent overheating in hot weather, raise humidity by damping down hard greenhouse floors with water.

MINI-GREENHOUSE

A tent-like structure with shelves and a plastic zip-up cover. The shelves can cast shade, which is not ideal for seedlings, but mini-greenhouses are still useful in the same way unheated greenhouses are.

COLD FRAME

A glass or plastic box with a sloped lid. Can be used in the same way as an unheated greenhouse (see above). Also useful in protecting overwintering plants.

Windowsills

For those with no outdoor space, windowsills offer the chance to grow your own. And for those with a garden but no greenhouse, they provide valuable space to raise seedlings in the early part of the season, when outdoor temperatures are too cold.

The pleasure of growing something comes from the journey, not the yield, but even on a windowsill you can maximize the space by hanging plants from above. The current craze for house plants means a huge selection of hanging pots are available, which can be suspended from hooks or a rail. Not all have drainage holes, so ensure you grow plants in pots that do and place these inside the hanging pot. The same effect can be achieved with tin cans, yogurt pots and plastic bottles (cut in half with the lid at the base), with drainage holes made in the bottom. Take the pots down to water or it will be messy. Avoid having too many hanging or you'll block the light to any plants below.

See overleaf for tips on how to get the best from your sill, and a list of plants that are suitable candidates.

← Chives, mint, violas and baby beetroot will all grow well on a windowsill.

Grow Easy windowsill plants

For individual growing information, varieties and pot sizes, see Top 30 spotlights from page 110 onwards. Salad leaves sown in late August/September provide winter pickings, cropped as cut-and-come-again leaves (see page 148).

↑ Windowsill seedlings and plants need regular attention (see opposite).

PLANT	SUNNY SILL (MINIMUM 6 HOURS SUN PER DAY)	SUNNY OR SEMI-SHADED SILL (MINIMUM 4 HOURS SUN PER DAY)	WINTER HARVEST POSSIBLE
HERBS			
Basil	*		
Chives		*	*
Mint		*	*
Parsley		*	*
Thyme	*		*
SALAD			
Asian leaf mix, cut-and-come-again lettuce or 'Little Gem'		*	*
Chard (baby)		*	*
Kale (baby)		*	*
Rocket (baby)		*	*
Spinach (baby)		*	*
Summer purslane (baby)	*		
MICROGREENS			
Greek cress		*	*
Pea shoots		*	*
Red mustard		*	*
VEGETABLES			
Beetroot (baby)	*		
Carrot (baby)	*		
Radish	*		
Tomato (windowsill type)	*		
FLOWERS			
Calendula	*		
Rose geranium	*		*
Viola	*		*
FRUIT			
Alpine strawberry	*		

Windowsill tips & tricks

These indoor ledges can prove tricky environments for plants, but get it right and you'll be adding little bursts of flavour to your plate year-round.

LIGHT

Even on sunny sills, the light is much reduced compared with outside or in a greenhouse. Low light, coupled with warmth (often from central heating) leads to leggy, or spindly, seedlings and plants, which grow tall and floppy in their search for the sun. This produces weak plants that can't stand up to outside conditions or pests and diseases.

Choose your sunniest sill for Top 30 plants. Ideally, it should be south-facing and receive at least six hours of sunlight a day. But be aware that these sills can get very hot at midday, so be sure to offer shade to young plants to prevent scorching. Next best is east-facing, with bright morning light. Certain

↑ A leggy viola plant reaches for the light.

herbs and baby leafy salads can succeed on shadier sills (see chart opposite). If you have only a north-facing sill, then stick to microgreens and consider LED grow lights, which can be found cheaply online. These can also be useful for raising seedlings in spring when the days are shorter, although simply sowing later may be a better option (see The Juggle, page 25).

HEAT

Seeds need heat to germinate but seedlings and plants need cooler conditions in order to grow on. Too much heat can lead to legginess. Be wary of radiators by windowsills, and open windows to ventilate if needed. See Windowsill seedlings, page 25, for further information and advice.

← Brush your hand over indoor seedlings and plants to toughen them up.

TURNING

Turn seedlings 180 degrees every day to straighten up their stems, and larger plants a few times a week. If you have several rows of plants, rotate the front and back rows weekly. Don't overcrowd your sill – plants will compete for light.

POT SIZE

As long as you make drainage holes in your pots, you can use a range of containers, from recycled tin cans to yogurt pots (see page 15). But the size of container you choose will have a big effect on plant growth. Where possible, bigger is always better for established plants. See my Top 30 spotlights (page 110), for suggested pot sizes.

COMPOST

Plants dry out quickly on sunny windowsills. I've found peat-free, wool-based potting compost holds water and nutrients best in containers.

TOUCH

Get tactile! Brush your hands over seedlings and small plants to toughen them up. This mimics the breeze outside and encourages a thicker, more anchored stem.

WATER

Windowsill plants dry out very quickly. Check daily for watering (see page 35). To avoid getting water on your sill, stand pots on saucers or baking trays.

PEST PATROL

Pesky aphids, whitefly and fungus gnats often move in on windowsill plants, and there are no predatory insects inside your home to gobble them up. If feasible, open the window as much as possible to allow beneficial insects to find their way in (see page 80–1 for solutions). Good airflow is also important to prevent fungal diseases, such as damping off (see page 83).

→ Resist sowing seeds too early to avoid major congestion on your windowsill.

IN DEPTH: WINDOWSILL SEEDLINGS

Some homes are cooler than others, and seeds have different requirements. Tomatoes, courgettes, French and runner beans and winter squashes all need warmer temperatures to germinate (check my Top 30 spotlights , page 110 for information). If you're struggling to get things going, here are some backups:
* Use a heated windowsill propagator or waterproof warming mats (use propagator lids that sit over seed trays to retain moisture). Ensure the lids are vented and remove once the seedlings have emerged. Prick out and remove seedlings as soon as possible.
* The seeds in my Top 30 don't need light for germination so just pick the warmest spot in your house or near a radiator. Put trays or pots in a plastic bag to retain moisture, and as soon as seedlings have sprouted remove the bag and move them to light.

The juggle

Inevitably, windowsill growing leads to the gardener's juggle: space in your home is maxed out, seedlings are leggy and need to go outside but it is too cold, anxiety levels rise! To limit stress, hold off sowing Top 30 plants on your sill until late March when light levels pick up. (Tomatoes to be grown in greenhouses should be sown by mid-March latest.)

Seedlings can then be hardened off otside (see page 66) on sunny days in mid- to late spring to toughen them up and provide extra light. But remember that frost-sensitive plants can't be planted outside until mid- to late May, once all danger of frost has passed.

If you don't have a suitable windowsill, it's possible to skip the indoor sowing (see the direct sowing calendar, page 95).

Top windowsill crop: *Microgreens*

↑ Easy-to-grow red mustard microgreens.

Microgreens get my vote for the easiest, tastiest windowsill crop. They are the dainty seedlings of a range of vegetables and herbs, cropped with only a few sets of leaves. Surprisingly flavourful and nutritious for their size, most dishes are enlivened with a sprinkle of these pretty leaves. They offer quick returns and year-round harvests.

They are happiest on sunny sills, but will grow in a shadier position, where they will be leggier but still flavourful.

If you're planning on growing a continuous supply, buy bulk seed. You only get one crop with microgreens (except for pea shoots, which have a second flush). However, if this is the only thing you are growing, it is worth it.

MY FAVOURITE MICROGREENS

For easy home growing: red mustard, Greek cress, pea shoots

For winter harvesting: kale, red mustard, pea shoots, red cabbage, pak choi, rocket – these will be slower to grow than summer crops

For something unusual: red amaranth, nasturtium, 'Rambo' radish, shiso, sunflower shoots, lemon basil

---

Sowing microgreens step-by-step

What you'll need:

Peat-free, organic, multipurpose potting compost

Seed trays or recycled plastic food trays

Piece of wood, notebook or similar, to fit shape of tray

Seeds

Plant label

Watering can with rose or homemade spray bottle (see page 69)

Sharp knife or scissors

1 Break up any lumps in the potting compost and fill the trays, ideally to a depth of 5cm (2in), the size of a standard seed tray, although as little as 3cm (1in) can work. If using repurposed trays, make sure they have drainage holes.

2 Firm down the compost with something flat that fits the shape of the tray, such as a piece of wood or a notebook. Press lightly to create an even surface.

3 Empty the packet of seeds into your hand, then sprinkle liberally on top of the compost for a more controlled, even covering – you don't want any bare patches but you don't want too many seeds touching either.

5 Water the tray carefully until it feels heavy using a rose on a watering can so that the seeds are not displaced. Alternatively, you can sink plastic trays into water for a few minutes, with the water reaching halfway up the tray. Or use a homemade plastic watering bottle (see page 69).

4 Cover the seeds with a fine layer of compost. Label.

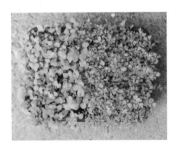

6 Place the trays on your sunniest windowsill. Keep the compost moist by watering every 1–2 days once the seedlings unfurl their first set of leaves. (see Windowsill tips & tricks, pages 22–5).

7 Microgreens are ready to crop when the first leaves appear. But I prefer to wait for the second set of leaves, to get more bang for my buck. Take a sharp knife or scissors and crop just above soil level. Use them straightaway.

8 You can reuse most of the compost – just scrape off the top 5–10mm (about ¼in) and top up with a bit of fresh compost before sowing another crop.

Window boxes

↓ This homemade wooden box is perfect for growing Mediterranean herbs, such as sage and rosemary.

Window boxes make it possible to grow food in an apartment, perhaps many storeys up! There are plenty of window boxes available to buy, or you can fashion your own from wooden crates or drawers, but ensure you give them drainage holes.

Containers are heavy when planted up, so make sure your sill can support them. In exposed spots, make sure that a box cannot be dislodged by wind. Consider metal brackets bolted to the wall, or hooks and eyes with a sturdy wire to hold it in place. Fill with peat-free, organic, multipurpose potting compost, leaving a 3cm (1in) gap at the top. All window boxes dry out fast and need daily watering. I use a wool-based compost to retain moisture and mulch the surface with garden or worm compost.

WHAT SIZE WINDOW BOX?

This will depend on your ledge or sill, but the following should be kept in mind.

* Minimum dimensions: L50cm (20in) × W20cm (8in) × H18–20cm (7–8in)
* Optimum dimensions: L1m (39in) × W30cm (12in) × H20cm (8in)
* Smaller window boxes are available but they dry out fast.

Best window box crops from my Top 30

For individual varieties, see Top 30 spotlights, starting on page 110.

VEGETABLES

Tomatoes (trailing/tumbling or compact bush varieties), chard, beetroot, dwarf kale, radish, salad leaves, carrots, dwarf runner beans, dwarf French beans.

FLOWERS

Calendula, viola, French marigolds, nasturtium, rose geranium.

FRUIT

Strawberry, alpine strawberry.

HERBS

All the herbs in my Top 30 will grow in a window box, but the best options are: basil, chives, parsley, rosemary, sage and thyme. Mint will take over, so only grow one variety by itself.

SHADY SILLS

Salads, chives, parsley, sorrel, chervil.

HOT SILLS

Tomatoes, rosemary, sage, thyme, summer purslane, rose geranium.

DESIGN COMBINATIONS

Choose taller, eye-catching plants for the back of the box, compact 'filler' plants for the middle, and trailing plants for the front that will spill over the edges. Top 30 plants are listed in each category on pages 38–9.

MORE COMBINATIONS

Mediterranean: thyme, purple sage, prostrate (trailing) rosemary and creeping thyme.
Salad: lettuce, parsley, violas.
Winter: Asian greens, land cress, chervil.

LARGE BOX

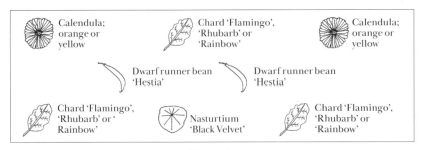

L1m (39in) x W30cm (12in) x H20cm (8in)

MEDIUM BOX

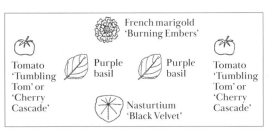

L50cm (20in) x W20cm (8in) x H18–20cm (7–8in)

Pots

All the crops in this book grow well in pots. Arguably, container growing is easier than growing in the ground – you aren't battling to improve the soil because you can use good-quality potting compost, and you can move pots into the optimum positions for particular crops. A colourful miscellany of edible crops in pots will give any ornamental garden a run for its money, luring in pollinators and providing delicious food.

← An assortment of pots and plants, including calendula, lettuce, chard, rosemary, mint and kale.

Choosing your container

↑ Plants thrive in a mix of pots, including an old tin bath – remember the drainage holes!

With the right dimensions, drainage and decent compost, more or less any container will do for growing. I use old sinks, baths, chimney pots, animal feed troughs and milk pails, all collected from various salvage yards. I've even grown potatoes in compost sacks and rhubarb in dustbins.

WHAT SIZE POT?

Generally, bigger is always better. If space, weight and cost are not an issue, opt for larger pots of 20 litres (5¼ gallons) capacity for most crops. Salads and herbs will be fine in 5–10 litres (1⅓–2½ gallons) outside, and even in 1-litre pots (1¾ pint) pots on an indoor windowsill. Squash and potatoes will thrive in 40 litres (10½ gallons). For fruit trees,

consider 40 litres (10½ gallons) a minimum; go large. Not all pots will correspond to this chart exactly, so if you're a few centimetres out either way, don't worry. Similarly, makeshift containers may not fit any of these dimensions but use them as a guide.

The volume of a pot is more important than the height alone. It's no good growing a plant in a nice deep container that is very narrow, as the overall volume may be inadequate. Try to ensure the pot has a good, open circumference.

Choose larger pots with a mix of plants growing in them, as opposed to lots of little, individual ones. Small pots will dry out much quicker and require more watering.

See Top 30 spotlights, page 110 – pot sizes are listed for each crop, as well as how many plants you can fit per pot.

Consider the final weight of your planted pots if they are to be placed on a roof or balcony. A large container of wet compost is heavy. Consult a structural engineer if you have any concerns.

POT DIMENSIONS

POT SIZE	POT HEIGHT	POT DIAMETER (TOP)
1 litre (1¾ pints)	11cm (4in)	13cm (5in)
5 litres (1⅓ gallons)	18cm (7in)	22.5cm (9in)
10 litres (2½ gallons)	22.5cm (9in)	28cm (11in)
15 litres (4 gallons)	30cm (12in)	33cm (13in)
20 litres (5¼ gallons)	32.5cm (13in)	35.5cm (14in)
40 litres (10½ gallons)	45cm (18in)	50cm (20in)

CONTAINER MATERIALS

What your container is made from will affect how your plants grow and how you take care of them.

CONTAINER TYPE	PROS	CONS
Terracotta	Adds charm to any garden, and improves with age As water evaporates through clay, the pots create a cooling effect, preventing the plants from overheating If looked after, terracotta pots will last many years	Heavy Need frequent watering Pricey – look for secondhand pots Can crack in frost. Look for frostproof terracotta or, in cold areas, move into a frost-free place or lift up off the ground with bricks
Plastic	Lightweight Cheap Requires less watering	Negative environmental impact – source recyclable pots and/or reuse pots Not aesthetically pleasing – hide them at the back of displays Blows over more easily due to its light weight
Metal	Durable Good-looking	Overheats in hot weather – line with recycled bubble wrap or cardboard to help insulate roots
Wood (for more on wood see Raised beds page 41)	Beautiful Natural	Untreated wood gradually rots when left outside – use bricks to raise containers off the ground and line them with old compost sacks, pricked with drainage holes
Fabric vegetable planter bags	Roots are 'air pruned' by the fabric which stops pot-bound plants Made from recycled materials Lightweight Fold flat when not in use, and are reusable	Sides are not as sturdy as other materials Dry out faster than plastic pots
Grow bags (plastic)	Fit well into small spaces Cheap (however, many do not include quality compost – look for peat-free, organic)	Shallow with limited soil volume – fewer nutrients are available so plants will need feeding regularly More watering needed as they dry out fast – increase soil volume for large plants like tomatoes by using a few tricks (see * below) Plastic is unsustainable and the bag can only be used once, but you can reuse compost from spent bags to top-dress other pots

*You can increase the volume in grow bags by using two bags, one on top of the other: cut a long rectangle out of the top of one bag, then place a second bag directly on top – use a sharp knife to cut out the base of the top bag to allow roots to grow into the bottom bag. Another option is to buy 'ring-culture' pots to insert into a grow bag, or make your own by cutting the base out of a 22cm (9in) diameter plastic pot with secateurs. Cut holes in the top of the grow bag and push the pots into position, then plant into the pots and fill with extra potting compost.

Filling pots

Choosing what to fill your pots with can be difficult. There are two options: a soil-based mix or a multipurpose compost.

When I worked in professional gardens, I was taught to use soil-based mixes in containers, specifically ones rich in nutrients such as John Innes No.3, which is available to buy in bags. This mimics normal soil better than multipurpose compost, but it's not available organically so I don't buy it for home use.

You could make your own with bought-in loam, garden compost and organic fertilizers, like seaweed meal and rock dust, but in the interests of 'grow easy', keep reading!

Organic, peat-free, multipurpose potting compost works well for me (I'm talking about bagged compost, not homemade garden/kitchen compost). It can dry out more than a soil-based mix, but it's lightweight, so more suitable for balconies or rooftops. It pays to invest in quality compost with the Soil Association stamp.

Don't take a short cut and fill your pots with garden soil alone – there simply won't be enough nutrients.

Blueberries need acidic soil to grow successfully – standard multipurpose compost is too alkaline and they will become gradually weaker. Luckily acidic potting compost is available to buy called 'ericaceous' compost.

When potting up, leave a 3cm (1in) gap between the compost and the top of the pot to allow for watering.

See also Feeding Pots, page 36, for advice on top-dressing pots.

↑ Beetroot growing in organic, peat-free, multipurpose compost.

Watering pots

↑ Direct water to the compost at the roots, as opposed to watering the leaves from above.

* Plants in pots dry out far quicker than those in the ground. Check pots daily, especially in warm weather. Pop a finger into the compost up to your second knuckle, checking for moisture under the surface. Sometimes the compost looks dry on top but is damp below.
* If you have lots of pots, a hose with a spray gun rose attachment is a good investment to save you time refilling watering cans.
* A rainwater butt is a must if you have the space.
* The smaller the pot, the more quickly the compost will dry out – use larger pots where possible.
* Water in the morning. Watering at night means plants are sat in wet, cool compost – slug heaven!
* If morning isn't possible, early evening is preferable to the middle of the day, when water quickly evaporates.
* Give pots a good soak at each watering, as opposed to the little-and-often approach. Fill the pot up and let it drain a few times – the compost should be moist, not soggy.
* Watering will likely be a daily job in the summer.
* Wind is drying, so stay alert on windy days.
* If your pots look waterlogged, check the drainage holes aren't blocked. Using 'crocks' (broken pieces of terracotta) to partially cover the holes can prevent this.
* Water the compost as opposed to the leaves, directing it to the base of the plant near the roots.
* If the pots are in full sun, cluster them together, creating edges of dappled shade, which can be beneficial.
* If you make your own compost (garden or worm), use a 1.5–2cm (½–¾in) layer to top-dress pots. This will help to lock in moisture (don't push the compost right up to the stem or it can cause rot).

Feeding pots

↑ Plants growing in pots generally need regular feeding.

✳ Plants need a mix of nutrients, particularly nitrogen (N) for leaf growth, phosphorus (P) for root growth and potassium (K) for fruit growth.

✳ The back of the compost bag tells you how long the nutrients will last – most will be six weeks. After that, apply organic liquid feed to the base of plants from April until the end of August, or September if you are growing winter crops. There's no need to feed in winter, as growth will be limited.

✳ Some compost brands have enough nutrients to last a year without feeding (see Resources, pages 220–1).

✳ As a general rule, feed every two weeks, but observe and adjust if necessary. Little and often is better than big hits with feeding.

✳ There are various organic liquid feeds available. I favour organic seaweed feed – it's like a vitamin pill for plants, offering a range of nutrients.

✳ Always feed when the compost is moist. Plants can't take up nutrients in dry compost, and the feed will simply drain out of the pot. Always follow the instructions on the bottle.

✳ Making your own feed is cheaper and more sustainable (see page 70).

✳ You can also replenish pots with garden or worm compost, top-dressing them with a layer about 1.5cm (½in) deep, or dig in some fermented bokashi (see page 58) or well-rotted manure for hungry crops. If top-dressing, don't push the compost right up to the plant stems because it can cause them to rot.

✳ A few handfuls of rock dust (full of minerals) will also benefit pots (see Resources, pages 220–1).

How to plant a container step-by-step

What you'll need

Tin bath, measuring around L70cm (28in) × W50cm (20in) × H30cm (12in)

Drill

Crocks

Organic, peat-free multipurpose potting compost

Homemade garden or worm compost (optional)

Trowel (optional)

3 × 'Flamingo' chard

1 × 'Dwarf Green Curled' kale

1 × 'Red Russian' kale

2 × calendula

Butterfly netting (optional)

1 Use a drill to make drainage holes in the tin bath. Space them evenly across the base – there is no ideal number.

2 I always use crocks (broken pieces of terracotta) to roughly cover the holes. This prevents them clogging with compost and aids drainage.

3 Fill your container with the compost, leaving a 3cm (1in) gap between the compost and the rim. If you plan to top-dress with your own compost, you can leave an additional 1–2cm (¼–¾in). Pull back the compost with your hand or a trowel to the depth of the root of the young plant or seedling. Insert the plant in the hole. Draw the compost back around the roots and press down lightly, to firm in. If plants are leggy (floppy), sink them in deeper, up to the first set of leaves.

4 Space the plants evenly in the container. The chard and kale provide small- to medium-sized leaves in this planting, while the calendula provides edible flowers.

5 Once planted, top-dress with 1.5cm (½in) of garden or worm compost. Water well, and once the nutrients have been used up in the compost, start a feeding regime (see page 36). If planting kale, insert canes and drape over butterfly netting, or check daily for caterpillars and pick off.

Looking good

With handy design combinations up your sleeve, pots with plants that are edible *and* beautiful are easy to achieve.

Garden designers often refer to thriller, filler and spiller plants when planting containers. Thriller 'impact' plants are positioned towards the back, compact fillers in the middle, and plants that tumble over edges at the front.

As well as looking good, plants are often happier in polycultures (the opposite of monocultures), where two or more different plants grow together in the same space. They occupy different niches, while simultaneously benefiting each other. This could be as simple as tomatoes and French marigolds in a pot, where marigolds support the tomatoes by attracting pollinators and potentially repelling whitefly. Lower-growing plants can also suppress weeds and protect the soil. Odd numbers of plants look best in containers – think in threes, fives and sevens.

DESIGN COMBINATIONS

Opt for nice wide pots. Plant fillers and spillers in gaps and edges – not directly under taller plants. Alternatively, cluster individual pots together with thrillers at the back.

1. Kale or cavolo nero, with dwarf French/dwarf runner beans (beans provide nitrogen for leafy kale through nodules on their roots). An undersowing of a white clover green manure does the same trick. Compact nasturtium, calendula and salad leaves also look lovely beneath kale. Ensure the kale has a 3- to 4-week head start.
2. Apple tree, 1 or 2 runner beans to climb the tree (provided the apple is not too young and has an open structure), compact nasturtium (which can repel woolly aphids) or edge the pot with chives (which, reportedly, results in less scab disease).
3. Climbing French beans, underplanted with lettuce or Asian mix salad (salad enjoys the dappled shade in summer and the nitrogen provided by the beans).
4. Carrots, with chives (repelling carrot fly) to edge the pot.
5. Climbing squash, underplanted with nasturtiums, calendula or French marigolds (draw in pollinators to aid fruiting).
6. Alpine strawberries, purple sage and garlic chives. A very pretty combination when chives are in flower, and the strong scent of sage and chives can confuse pests that might be attracted to the sweet-smelling strawberries.

See some ideas for window box combinations on page 29. These can also be adapted to big pots.

→ Nasturtiums growing beneath the leaves of kale 'Nero di Toscana'.

IMPACT (THRILLERS)

Apple tree

Beetroot 'Bull's Blood'

Calendula

Chard ('Flamingo', 'Rainbow', 'Rhubarb')

French marigold

Kale

Rose geranium

Tomatoes (tall/cordon)

'Tromboncino' squash (trained up a support)

Winter squash/pumpkin (small-fruited varieties to train up a support, such as 'Delicata', 'Jack-Be-Little', 'Sweet Dumpling')

COMPACT (FILLERS)

Basil (purple, Greek, cinnamon)

Chives (common, garlic)

Dwarf French/runner beans ('Helios', 'Purple Tepee', 'Hestia')

Kale ('Peacock White/Red', dwarf varieties)

Lettuce (see page 147 for varieties)

Parsley

Rosemary (when small)

Sage (when small)

Tomatoes ('Tumbling Tom', 'Cherry Cascade')

GROUND COVER

Alpine strawberries

Baby salad leaves (see page 152)

Chervil

Pea shoots

Radish

Thyme (creeping)

Viola

CASCADING (SPILLERS)

Dwarf runner beans ('Hestia')

Nasturtium ('Black Velvet', 'Empress of India')

Rosemary (prostrate)

Strawberry

Raised beds

This book is all about making things easy, and raised beds do just that. Later in the book you'll find a crop plan for two raised beds, of 1.2 × 2.4m (4 × 8ft), that provide a succession of crops from spring to winter (see page 96).

↑ A raised bed, 1.2 × 2.4m (4 × 8ft), pictured in early summer.

Raised beds come in many forms, with or without sides to hold the soil/compost in place. I recommend beds with sides. They are tidy and allow for a good depth of soil from the start.

The sides can be made of wood, recycled plastic boards (specifically for raised beds), brick or galvanized metal. None are perfect, but wood is my first choice.

There's a lot to consider when choosing your wood. Do you choose untreated or pressure-treated (tanalized) timber? Treated timber will last far longer, but there is a chance that chemicals may leach into the soil (more on this below).

↑ The sides of this raised bed are made of untreated oak.

PROS OF RAISED BEDS

They instantly solve the problems of a challenging soil as you are importing your own mix of compost and/or topsoil into beds at a good depth.

They create a neat growing area.

No-dig raised beds, which I recommend (see page 44), save preparation time as you can build them straight onto your lawn without removing any grass.

Compost/well-rotted manure can be applied in a targeted way, exactly where you need it for higher fertility.

There is no need to walk on raised beds, so you will have no problems with soil compaction.

CONS OF RAISED BEDS

Cost of materials – you'll need to buy wood (or similar) and soil/compost mix to fill the beds.

Pests – some people report more damage from slugs, as they can lurk down the sides of a raised bed, but I have never found this to be an issue.

UNTREATED WOOD

In an ideal world, using a sustainably sourced hardwood native to your country is best. Hardwood has longevity and doesn't require treatment. Oak is a good choice. You can use a natural preservative like linseed to extend its life. The downside is cost, which may be prohibitive if you're making · lots of beds.

← Untreated scaffolding boards form the sides of these raised beds.

If you choose treated timber, there are a few steps you can take to help prevent chemicals leaching into the soil:

✳ Allow the timber to dry out for a few weeks before installing it, preferably in warm, sunny weather.
✳ Line the inside of raised beds with black plastic – ensure it's porous, like a landscaping fabric, to prevent waterlogging.

If building beds on soil or grass, don't line the bottom, otherwise worms and other microorganisms won't be able to get in! Staple the liner to boards and overlap onto the soil inside the base of the bed by 15cm (6in).

Whether the wood is treated or untreated, look for the Forest Stewardship Council (FSC), Programme for the Endorsement of Forest Certification (PEFC) or the Soil Association (SA) mark (in the UK).

Using softwoods that are untreated, such as larch, means the wood will rot more quickly. However, it should still last several seasons, by which time you could remove it – the soil beneath will now be good and excess compost can be spread elsewhere. Using reclaimed wood or builder's scaffolding planks is also an option, as long as you know the wood hasn't been treated with anything nasty.

TREATED WOOD

Treated timber is available from builder's merchants. The Soil Association (the UK's largest organic certification body) states that if the timber used for organic vegetable beds is pre-treated with preservative (for example, with Tanalith E), then this doesn't affect organic status. Products today are less harmful than those used in the past, which contained arsenic. But the SA doesn't allow you to treat wood yourself with a synthetic preservative.

Filling beds

Unless your bed is very small, bagged multipurpose compost from the garden centre won't cut it. It's more cost effective to buy your chosen medium in bulk. Consider what you can get hold of locally and let this guide you. I've filled beds with various mediums – all the following work well:

* Well-rotted manure only.
* Municipal green waste compost, mushroom compost or garden compost topped up with well-rotted manure.
* Topsoil, pre-blended with organic matter (such as multipurpose compost or manure) is available to buy in bulk. Be sure to check the source for any additions – you don't want it enriched with synthetic fertilizers or peat. For a cheaper option, buy pure topsoil and make your own additions. Choose 'premium' topsoil to British Standard BS3882:2015. When filling a bed, stop 8cm (3in) from the top. Top the bed up with 5cm (2in) of garden compost, peat-free multipurpose compost, or well-rotted manure, and mix it into the top layer.

WELL-ROTTED MANURE

If well rotted, this should look like compost and not smell of manure. It should have been left for at least a year before using. Horse manure is a better all-rounder than cow manure, but cow manure is higher in nutrients for hungry soils. Chicken manure is richest in nutrients and best used sparingly – add it to the compost heap to rot down first.

Ask what the animals are fed and what medication they may have been given. Beware of contamination from the weedkiller Aminopyralid in horse manure as it distorts growth and kills tomatoes, potatoes and beans – check the hay the horses have been fed has not been sprayed with it.

GREEN WASTE COMPOST

Always look for PAS100 certification to indicate its quality standard (in UK) and beware of contaminants like sharp metal and plastics. (In the US see www.compostingcouncil. org.) Green waste compost can be hot on arrival and may need longer to compost and cool – if using it instead of topsoil, top-dress it with 5cm (2in) of well-rotted manure, as it is not a nutrient-rich medium.

MUSHROOM COMPOST

A by-product of the mushroom-growing industry. Light and crumbly with average nutrient levels, it can contain manure, straw and chalk (chalk can make some batches more alkaline). If using on alkaline soils you may want to alternate it with another medium each year. It is thought a high pH can inhibit growth, but I've created kitchen gardens successfully on alkaline soils.

Building your raised bed

A note before starting...

I favour the no-dig approach, pioneered by the organic vegetable gardener Charles Dowding in the UK. Digging the soil disturbs the delicate balance of microorganisms and throws weed seeds to the surface. 'No dig' leaves the soil below undisturbed and is accompanied by mulching with organic matter on top, such as garden compost, multipurpose compost, green waste, mushroom compost or well-rotted manure. You then sow or plant into the mulch as opposed to the soil below, protecting its structure.

Applying this to raised beds means you can build them straight onto your lawn or current beds, without digging the ground over first. As little as 15cm (6in) of mulch straight onto your lawn will kill the grass (but remove any perennial weeds first, see opposite).

For beginners, I suggest a minimum depth of 25cm (10in); this allows the plants to establish themselves quickly and be off to a flying start.

Beds built onto hard surfaces need to be deeper than they would on soil. A minimum depth of 45–60cm (1½–2ft) is preferable. Porous plastic raised bed liners are available as a quick drainage fix. Worms and beneficial organisms need importing with garden compost/rotted manure, or even a little garden soil.

Paths

Allow 45–60cm (1½–2ft) for paths between beds. If building raised beds onto lawn, you can strim the paths for easy maintenance or mulch them with compost or woodchips over landscaping fabric.

↑ Constructing a 1.2 × 2.4m (4 × 8ft) bed with 25cm (10in) height oak boards. Railway sleepers also work well. Their standard length is 2.4m (8ft), so three sleepers will build you a 1.2 × 2.4m (4 × 8ft) bed. However, I don't recommend sleepers if you are following the crop plan on page 96. Avoid old, reclaimed railway sleepers, which contain toxic creosote. See pages 41–2 for other wooden side options. Note, this bed is built straight onto lawn. Often a layer of cardboard is used to cover the grass first, but at this depth the mulch alone will suppress its growth.

↑ Use a trowel to remove any perennial weeds – see page 87 to identify these.

↑ Use square batons hammered into the ground for screwing the boards on to. Position the bed in a sunny spot, orientated to suit your space. North–south, east–west or as near as are all fine. Just be aware that with east–west plantings, taller crops cast shade on their northern edge at midday.

← Fill the bed with your chosen growing media (topsoil/compost/manure – see page 13) up to 3cm (1in) from the top. You can plant straightaway. For two 1.2 × 2.4m (4 × 8ft) beds needed for the crop plan, you will need roughly 1½ bulk bags of medium to fill the beds.

No-dig systems will require an annual top-up of 3–5cm (1–2in) of your chosen compost in winter.

How to grow

Plants want to grow. They just need their roots in fertile ground and a little help from you. This chapter will arm you with the basics to grow healthy, vibrant crops. Do remember, despite your nurture, crops sometimes fail. Luckily, next season spins quickly around and you'll have another chance, battle-scarred but wiser!

Growing organically has always felt instinctive to me. Be present with your plants, enrich the ecosystem and you will be rewarded. There's a vitality to produce grown with natural methods that is hard to pin down, but it sure makes it tastes exceptional, and I want you to savour that too.

← Measuring up before planting multi-sown beetroot plugs.

Why grow organic?

Our planet is in crisis. Now more than ever we need to produce food in an environmentally friendly way without reliance on synthetic, petroleum-based fertilizers and pesticides. We need to replace lost wildlife habitats and nurture our soils, which are not only our lifeblood, but also have the capacity to store carbon. Stored carbon in our soils has the potential to lower atmospheric CO_2 – a primary driver of climate change. Regenerative farmers are practising techniques to support this and reverse soil degradation, but we can contribute on a home scale too.

By growing your own organically, you can take control of your food (at least some of it) and play your part in conserving this beautiful earth. Whatever the size of your plot, you can become the guardian of your little patch and create a robust ecosystem, humming with life. Even on a windowsill you'll be amazed at the insect friends that come and go when you leave the window open.

Research has highlighted that organically grown crops are up to 60 per cent higher in a number of key antioxidants. Combine this with the benefits of being outside with your hands in the soil, and growing this way feels good.

The perils of pests, diseases and unpredictable weather present challenges to any vegetable grower. But with the right knowledge, which you'll glean from these pages, growing organically is a simple practice.

↑ Squash 'Sweet Dumpling' with a trailing nasturtium.

What is organic growing?

Here are five key 'organic' principles and how to put them into practice.

1
CONSERVE & INCREASE SOIL LIFE

Use compost and green manures to feed and protect the soil, using no artificial fertilizers and always minimizing bare ground.

Practise no-dig growing (see page 44).

2
BUILD HEALTHY, DIVERSE ECOSYSTEMS

A garden full of different plants and wildlife will be productive and resilient. Grow diverse flowering plants to encourage beneficial insects, and create a healthy habitat for wildlife (see pages 61, 82).

3
AVOID TOXIC CHEMICALS (CHEMICAL WEEDKILLERS, PESTICIDES & FERTILIZERS)

Use natural methods of pest and disease control. Prevention is key.

Create healthy ecosystems (see page 60).

Outwit pests using barriers, traps and timings (see pages 71, 78–81).

Make your own feed (see page 70), and source peat-free, organic seed and potting compost (see Resources, pages 220–1).

Stay on top of weeds naturally (see page 86).

4
GOOD HUSBANDRY

Healthy spaces grow healthy plants. Keep tools and growing areas clean.

Ensure the seeds and plants you buy are from trusted suppliers (see Resources, pages 220–1). Even better, save your own seeds (see page 76).

Prioritize soil health (see page 50).

Know when to sow to give plants the best chances (see Top 30 spotlights, page 110).

5
CONSERVE RESOURCES

Be mindful of your use of water, energy, wood and plastics. Recycle, reuse, and aim to be as sustainable as possible in the choices you make for bought-in products like seeds, compost, tools and containers (see Resources, pages 220–1).

Start with soil

Soil is the living, breathing gut of the earth, where life begins and ultimately returns. It comprises a complex ecosystem of bacteria, fungi and other microorganisms. Look at a single pinch of healthy soil under a microscope – it will be teeming with life. Along with earthworms, soil microbes are vital in making nutrients available to plants and maintaining soil structure. The more diverse and plentiful they are, the better your garden will grow.

Our soils are rapidly degrading. Half the topsoil on the planet has been lost in the last 150 years, in part due to unsustainable agriculture. Globally we must regenerate the soil, and on a home scale the best way to do this is through making compost. This is even possible in a small space, thanks to wormeries (see page 58). As gardeners, we don't want to see bare ground open to the elements – we always want soil covered with diverse plants or compost.

Green manures – plants grown specifically to improve soil structure and fertility – are also a valuable resource for organic gardeners, especially those without enough materials or space to compost. They are sown, grown on and reincorporated back into the soil, adding nutrients. Mustard, trefoil, phacelia, crimson clover, buckwheat, vetch and rye are all good options (the last two covering bare ground over winter). Dig them back in to a depth of 15–18cm (6–7in) or (my preferred method for reduced soil disturbance) cut them down and cover with a light-excluding mulch, such as black polythene sheeting (for garden use) or cardboard. They rot down under the mulch, feeding the soil and leaving a clean area to plant in six weeks or so. Ensure they're reincorporated while still fresh and green, before they set seed.

Long-term green manures like white clover can be used to underplant fruit trees. Plants (like clover) in the legume family extract nitrogen from the air, making it available to other plants through nodules on their

← White clover can be grown as a green manure crop.

↑ Healthy soil supports vibrant crops, such as this mix of kale plants.

roots. Used as a 'living' mulch, clover can also suppress weeds and attract pollinators (for seed, see Resources, pages 220–1).

Soil health is still relevant if you're growing in pots. It means choosing a good-quality peat-free, organic, multipurpose potting compost and encouraging microorganisms with small-scale composting. Even quick-growing green manures like mustard, phacelia and crimson clover can be used.

Know your soil

Your garden may be on clay, sand, silt, loam, peat, chalk or a mix. Clay is heavy but high in nutrients. Sand is light and lower in nutrients. Silt is light, high in nutrients and compacts easily. Loam is a mix of clay, sand and silt – you're lucky if you have this! Peat is highly fertile and high in moisture. Chalk is high in lime and alkaline and can be heavy or light.

The ideal soil acidity is around pH 6.5, with most sources stating you need to be within the range of pH 5.5–7.5 to grow food. However, I created an abundant kitchen garden on clay loam soil with a pH of 8.2, so success is certainly possible on alkaline soils. If you're interested in your soil's makeup, you can buy home testing kits, but most soils can be improved with the addition of compost, well-rotted manure or green manure.

What is compost?

Here we're discussing homemade garden compost, not the bagged variety. Practically speaking, compost is decomposed organic matter – think plant-based food scraps, spent garden plants, twigs, cardboard, animal manures and weeds. On a deeper level, it's an artistic endeavour connecting you to the magical process of birth and decay.

If you enjoy baking, you'll enjoy composting, turning ingredients into something rich, fluffy and sweet smelling. If done right, there is no stink! Compost improves soil structure, adds nutrients and feeds soil life. It also acts as a mulch, protecting the soil underneath from erosion.

Turning compost speeds up the decomposition. It allows oxygen into the pile, which fuels a certain set of microorganisms to get busy and break it down, which generates heat as they digest the organic matter. Hot composting is appropriate when you generate a good amount of kitchen and garden waste and your bin fills quickly (needing to be turned). In small spaces you may not have space to turn or you may not produce much waste. But you don't *have* to have heat to make compost. Cold composting is when a heap or bin is left unturned. It will still break down but can take six months to a year to do so.

Space will largely dictate the type of compost you make but, rest assured, there are options for a range of growing situations which are outlined in the following pages.

↑ Homemade garden compost, five months old, which has been turned once.

Small- to medium-space composting

If your garden and kitchen both generate waste, then a compost heap is a good idea. Even small gardens may have space for one or two pallet compost bins. For instructions on how to build these, see overleaf. Bigger isn't always better – compost will break down more quickly in a full small compost bin than an empty big one.

If you don't fancy building your own, you can buy sealed compost bins that don't require turning and allow the compost to break down over time – you add to the top and collect from the bottom. Newer 'hot bin' inventions are well insulated, even allowing air in to speed up the process. Sealed bins are good where rats may be an issue.

For advice on composting in very small spaces, see page 58.

→ Old pallets can be used to make your compost bay.

How to build a pallet compost bin step-by-step

Start on a soil base if possible – you want soil life to migrate into your compost pile.

What you'll need:

3 recycled, untreated pallets (research your source beforehand – avoid spills, stains and coloured pallets and those marked with 'MB' – a toxic pesticide)

2 standard plywood sheets, to cover 4 sides

Electric drill

Long wood screws

Saw

I have three of these pallet bins alongside each other in my garden – a good system in a larger space. At any point, one is being added to, one is maturing and one is ready to go. As one bin fills, it is turned into the adjacent bin and ultimately used on beds or in pots. In a medium-sized space, two bins side by side would be ideal. But if this is a squeeze, one is still good.

1 Stand 3 pallets to form the sides of your compost bin and fix them together using long wood screws. Saw the sheets of ply to fit the inside (reserving a piece for the front). Screw each piece of ply to the inside of each pallet to create an open-fronted box. The ply is breathable, but allows enough heat to be generated, and conserves moisture.

2 Start filling your bin, placing any woody, twiggy material in first to help with air circulation.

3 Cut the remaining ply into several horizontal sections and screw them to the front in stages as you fill up the bin – this allows easy access and they can easily be unscrewed when you need to turn the compost. You need a front on the pile to generate enough heat.

ONE BIN?

Cold composting: leave the bin of compost unturned. It will break down slowly. You can let air into the pile (and speed up the process) by stirring with a garden fork, making holes in the pile with a hoe or rake handle, or buying a compost aerator tool. Adding chunky brown material, such as cardboard egg boxes and the inner tubes from toilet rolls, to allow air gaps also helps.

If the compost inside a sealed bin doesn't appear to be breaking down, locate a spot in your garden where you can place the contents and make a new pile. Empty out the bin, forking the top to the bottom of the new pile. Cover with a black polythene sheet and weigh down the sides. Allow to compost for a further three months or until it has broken down. At the same time, start again filling the original bin with your plant and kitchen waste.

TWO BINS?

Once full, allow the first bin to sit for a month, then turn the contents into the second bin, covering with a polythene sheet for another three months or more before using. Continue to fill the now empty bin.

Compost recipe

Good compost comprises green *and* brown material (see below). You may not generate enough materials yourself, which means sourcing, scrounging from neighbours and stockpiling. Making compost is not just about using up your plant waste – think of it as a recipe where you may need additional ingredients to make it sing.

INGREDIENTS

GREEN MATERIAL Grass clippings, food scraps, green leaves, weeds*, animal manures and coffee grounds (these look brown but are green and contain nitrogen). These are nitrogen-rich and moist in comparison to brown material.

   * Charles Dowding busted the myth for me that you can't include perennial weed roots – they *do* break down as long as they are well buried.

BROWN MATERIAL Paper and cardboard (without dyes), woody plant stems and twigs, straw, autumn leaves, woodchips and wood ash from the fire. These are carbon-rich ingredients.

OTHER INGREDIENTS Citrus and eggshells are fine to add, although wormeries don't like them, and eggshells do take an age to break down. Don't add meat or cooked foods to an open, outdoor pile, as this can attract rats. Rats also find dry piles more hospitable, so don't allow yours to dry out.

METHOD

Quantities don't have to be exact, but aim for a 50:50 ratio of green material to brown. Too much green and the pile will heat up rapidly, becoming wet and smelly. Naturally, your green layer will be a little deeper than the browns as greens tend to be more sizeable (compared to, say, a sheet of cardboard or some wood chippings).

Shred or chop up woody materials to aid a quicker breakdown. Cardboard can go in as complete sheets.

Roughly layer green and brown ingredients as available (keeping a permanent stack of brown next to the bin for easy access). The level will keep dropping, so once the bay is full, keep adding on top for a further few weeks.

Too much water/rainfall will make the pile soggy, leading to a lack of air needed by beneficial microbes. Cover with a piece of black polythene.

Conversely, in hot, dry weather, moisten any brown, woody layers and water the heap.

Compost should have the moisture content of a wrung-out sponge. Give it a squeeze – if more than a few drops come out, it's too wet. Add more brown material.

Hot composting

If you have enough material and space to turn, hot composting speeds things up. I aim for a temperature of 60°C (140°F) – hot enough to kill off weed seeds and diseases, but not so hot that it destroys beneficial microorganisms. A good range is 55–70°C (131–158°F) – get yourself a compost thermometer if you're serious!

Compost needs turning only *once* for faster decomposition. More turns are fine, but won't make vast improvements. My three-bay system allows for two turns and produces the good stuff – nicely broken down and smelling of earth. Once a bay is full, I let it sit for at least four weeks before turning. The final product has at least three months resting in its final bay (covered with black polythene) before use.

I don't sieve compost. Moving it into a wheelbarrow gives the chance to break up any lumps.

Mine generally contains some twiggy material that hasn't broken down (I don't have a shredder) but I spread this on beds, pulling out anything big to re-compost. If spread in winter, a lot of the lumps will be broken down by spring.

↑ Composting in progress – the bottom layer in the bin breaks down while new material is still being added to the top of the heap.

Very small-space composting

Composting your kitchen scraps in a small wormery (see Resources, pages 220–1), known as vermicomposting, is a good option for those with a small space. Worms produce beautiful compost from castings (their poo), which can be used to top-dress and feed plants. Liquid collects in the bottom of the wormery, known as 'worm tea', and is diluted with water (1 part to 10 parts water) as a liquid feed.

Composting worms are different from earthworms. Check instructions on what to feed them – generally kitchen vegetable scraps (no citrus, meat or dairy) and 25–30 per cent dry matter, like damp cardboard, paper and the inner tubes from toilet rolls. If kept correctly, you can have them indoors, but I once had escapees! A garden shed works well. No turning of material is required.

Bokashi is a Japanese composting system which ferments kitchen waste with an active bran. Suitable for container gardens or larger plots, it sits as a neat little bin in your kitchen. Microorganisms in the bran transform food waste into nutrient-rich pre-compost, which can be dug into soil, pots or compost heaps to break down further. Use the run-off as a liquid feed, diluting 1:100 with water.

↑ A compact wormery with three trays. Place the worms with bedding and food in the bottom tray. As this fills with worm castings, put food waste in the tray above. The worms will migrate up, leaving the usable worm compost in the layer beneath.

→ Composting worms in action.

Healthy ecosystems

↑ Flowering sage is a magnet for pollinators.

Your plants are connected to a bigger ecosystem, which needs to be in balance for them to flourish. Organic gardeners need to create diverse environments, where potential pest or disease issues are kept in check naturally.

Whether you're growing in a window box or have a garden, encouraging soil life, beneficial insects and wildlife will help your plants to thrive. Start from the ground up – soil supports all other life (see Start with soil, page 50).

Plant flowers between your vegetables to attract pollinators and predatory insects. There are some lovely flowering options in my Top 30 plants. Chives, lemon verbena, parsley (flowers in its second year), sage, rosemary, thyme, calendula, nasturtium, French marigolds, rose geranium, viola and strawberries. Plus glorious apple blossom in spring. And don't discount how helpful so-called weeds can be. Nettles, dandelions and rough, untended edges of lawns can provide important forage and habitat.

Welcome insects, birds, bats, small mammals, frogs, toads, newts and hedgehogs to your garden with bird baths, ponds and wood piles. Slugs may be a pain, but they're an important food source for some of these creatures. You may lose a small percentage of your food, but think of it as nurturing the bigger picture.

↑ **BUTTERFLIES AND MOTHS** These are important pollinators, as well as prey for birds and bats. Pictured is a peacock butterfly.

↑ **HOVERFLIES** Adult hoverflies feed on nectar and pollen, while the larvae eat aphids and other pests.

↑ **BEES** Bumblebees, honey bees and solitary bees are particularly important pollinators.

Beneficial insects

Insects often have a bad rap with gardeners, but the vast majority are harmless and many are beneficial. We need them for pollination, pest control and breaking down organic matter.

The following creatures are particularly helpful:

✳ Ground beetles: eat slugs and snails.
✳ Green lacewing adults: have transparent, lace-like wings and a pale green body. They eat aphids and insect eggs.

✳ Parasitic wasps: tiny wasps that don't sting. They lay their eggs on or inside the host insect, such as aphids. When hatched, the larvae eat the host alive; think *Alien*!
✳ Common wasps: important for pollination and pest control, feeding caterpillars and other insects to their grubs.

A diverse range of flowers, trees and shrubs will support beneficial insect life. This can be as simple as the pot-grown apples, blueberries, flowering herbs, edible flowers and vegetables mentioned in this book. See also Attracting beneficial insects on page 82.

↑ **LADYBIRDS** Adult ladybirds and their larvae feed on aphids (blackfly and greenfly). The larvae look like tiny, spiky crocodiles – black/grey, often with orange/red markings.

Sowing from seed

Most of my Top 30 crops can be sown from seed but there are a few exceptions and you will be waiting a rather long time for them to grow, so it's better to buy them. See Top 30 spotlights, page 110.

Seed can be sown directly into the ground where it is to grow (see page 68) or into pots, seed or module trays to plant out later. Wherever you sow, think of your seeds' needs, and provide warmth, moisture, air, good soil and light once germinated. See also Windowsill seedlings, page 25.

SEED SOWING DEPTH

For direct sowing outdoors, see page 68.

A general rule is to sow twice as deep as the seed is wide, but I prefer to use my finger as a guide. The majority of module-sown seeds in my Top 30 can be sown to the depth of the first knuckle on your index finger (1.5–2cm/½–¾in deep), aside from beans, which I sink to my second knuckle in pots.

Sowing a module tray step-by-step

Modules are my go-to for seed sowing. Exceptions are courgettes, squash and beans that need more space. I sow these straight into 9cm (3½in) pots. Even with no indoor space, you can still sow into modules on an outside table once the weather warms up (see the direct sowing guide on page 68).

What you'll need

Organic, peat-free seed compost

Module tray

Flat-edged piece of wood (optional)

Pencil

Seeds

Plant labels

Dustpan and brush (optional)

Watering can with a rose or hose with spray gun attachment

1 Break up any lumps in the compost.

2 Fill the module tray with compost, pushing it into individual cells with your fingers.

3 Put more compost on top, ensuring each cell is full.

4 Use a flat-edged piece of wood to brush off any remaining compost and create a flat surface; you can use your hand but it won't be as neat.

5 Make a hole with your finger or the top of a pencil (see Seed Sowing Depth, left).

6 Drop in the seed. If you are sowing a tray of different varieties, keep the holes uncovered until you've sown the whole tray, as it's easy to lose your place. Label as you go: vegetable, variety, date.

7 Close the holes with your fingers and add a small amount of compost on top to completely cover the holes. Use your flat-edged piece of wood to neaten the surface.

8 Keep the sowing area tidy to avoid confusion.

9 Moisture is needed for germination. Water using a watering can with a rose or a hose with a spray attachment. If you have neither, use a homemade water bottle (see page 69). Keep the compost damp until the seedlings emerge, then water regularly. Warmth is also needed for germination. Once germinated, seedlings need light – deprive them and they will become leggy (floppy).

Pricking out step-by-step

If you've sown your seeds in standard seed trays (not modules), there will come a point when you will need to prick out the seedlings to give them space to grow on. This just means easing your seedling out of the tray and moving it, roots intact, to a larger pot. Use 9cm (3½in) pots or equivalent (see Pots for seedlings & young plants, page 15) or for very small seedlings use even smaller pots or modules.

The time to prick out is when the second set of leaves have come through – these are called 'true leaves' – and the tray is getting crowded.

What you'll need:

Seed tray with seedlings showing second set of leaves

Watering can with a rose or hose with spray gun attachment

Pencil

Pots filled with organic, peat-free potting compost (9cm/3½in or similar)

Plant labels

1 Water the seed tray at least two hours before pricking out using a watering can with a rose, or a hose with a spray gun on the rose setting. You want moist (not wet) compost, so that the roots separate more easily. Insert a pencil into the compost beneath one of the seedlings, lifting a clump of soil to ease it out (it's fine if you lift out a small clump of seedlings; you can separate them). Always hold a seedling by its leaves, not the delicate stem that can bruise easily.

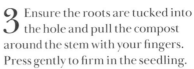

3 Ensure the roots are tucked into the hole and pull the compost around the stem with your fingers. Press gently to firm in the seedling.

2 Shake off a little of the compost from the roots, and make a hole in your prepared pot. Lower in the seedling, using the pencil to guide in the roots. If the stem is elongated and leggy, sink it up to its first leaves.

Thinning

If sowing straight into modules or small pots, always sow at least two seeds (per module or pot) as insurance, in case a seed doesn't germinate. This means hardening your heart and thinning to one seedling if both have got going.

Select the healthiest seedling to keep; if they are both the same, then it's pot luck which one stays! Use snips or scissors to cut the other seedling off at the base; don't pull it out, as this causes root disturbance to the remaining plant. And don't feel guilty; this way you're giving plants a chance to thrive.

4 Label and water.

← A multi-sown beetroot module, ready to be planted.

Potting on

This is the process of moving seedlings or small plants into larger pots to enable them to grow on with more space and nutrients. Tomatoes always need potting on, as they're started early and require warm weather before being planted out. Potting on can also be helpful if the bed or pot you'd earmarked is still cropping – it buys you time. For suitable pots, see page 15.

The time to pot on is when the rootball is holding the module firmly together and roots are poking out of the bottom of the module. Don't wait until the foliage starts to yellow. (See also Planting out, opposite).

* Water modules a few hours before potting on.
* Fill one-third of the pot with organic, peat-free multipurpose potting compost.
* Drop in the module, holding the leaves, not the stem. You want the top of the module to sit at soil level, unless it is a tomato, in which case you can sink it deeper (see Tomatoes, pages 154–8). If the seedling is leggy, sink it deeper, burying it up to the first set of leaves.
* Backfill with compost, leaving 1–2cm (¼–¾in) free at the top of the pot for watering, otherwise the soil spills over.
* Firm in the module – you want it to make contact with the new compost but not be compacted.

Hardening off

Hardening off allows plants to adjust gradually to conditions outdoors. Once temperatures allow, move plants out in the morning and in by the evening. After a week they will be acclimatized. Make sure you water plants before setting them outside to avoid giving them any additional stress. If you don't get a chance to harden plants off properly, horticultural fleece is an invaluable aid in protecting spring plantings (see page 71).

Planting out

Most seedlings from my Top 30 plants can be planted out in the ground as 'modules'. Others may have been started in pots or been potted on (like tomatoes), so are planted out as young plants.

* Plant into beds while the plants still look healthy. If they are in their modules or small pots for too long, their foliage will start to yellow as the nutrients run out.
* When roots appear through the bottom of the pot or module, begin to gently ease out the plant to check if it's ready for planting out – the rootball should hold together, not crumble. Sometimes a little squeeze of the pot or module is needed to release it.
* With a trowel, make a hole a little deeper and wider than the rootball and place the top of the root at soil level, unless it's a tomato, which can be sunk deeper (see page 155).

↑ Planting out runner beans to grow up a hazel tepee.

* Firm the soil gently around your plant using your fingers, and water well.
* If using barrier methods like netting or insect mesh to protect against pests, implement them immediately. If it's early in the year, use horticultural fleece for protection from the cold and wind (see page 71).

* For large plants, such as perennial herbs or fruit, you may need to break up the bottom of the planting hole with a hand fork if the ground feels compacted.
* If the plants are rootbound, trim the bottom of the roots with a sharp knife and tease them out so that they find their way into new compost.

← Direct sowing carrot seeds into a drill in a raised bed.

DRILL DEPTHS

Small seeds (carrots, lettuces): 2cm (¾in)

Large seeds (beans): 5cm (2in)

Inbetweeners (beetroot, kale, spinach): 3cm (1in)

Take small pinches of seeds, sprinkling them down the line swiftly and sparsely. Draw the soil back over the drill with a rake or your hand. The seeds and soil need to be in contact to allow the seeds access to moisture in the soil.

Sowing too thickly is common, which means more thinning. It takes practice to get right but you'll get a feel for it over time. See Top 30 spotlights, page 110, for final seed spacings.

Direct sowing

This refers to seed sown direct into the soil, as opposed to raising seedlings in pots or modules first. You can also sow direct into larger containers. I use modules for most Top 30 seeds, but carrots are best sown direct.

* Rake the soil to break up any hard lumps, creating a level surface. Make a taut line with string and sticks or pegs as a guide for your drill (a groove in the soil where you sow seeds).
* To make the drill, pull the edge of a trowel or the corner of a hoe through the soil, along the line. If the soil is soft, lay a rake or broom handle flat on its long edge, pressing it into the soil to make an indent.
* In dry weather, water the drill before sowing.

Watering

↑ A homemade watering bottle. Make holes in the lid with a skewer to create a gentle flow of water when the bottle is turned upside down.

Plants have different watering requirements – see Top 30 spotlights, page 110, for individual needs. Always be mindful of water usage, and collect rainwater if possible. See Watering pots, page 35.

GENERAL TIPS

Aim to water in the morning – damp, cool nights entice slugs and encourage fungal problems.

A thorough soaking less often is better than a little-and-often approach to watering.

As a general rule, leafy vegetables need more water than fruiting and rooting plants.

Overwatering is more problematic than under-watering. Too much water can lead to damping off disease (see page 83), and a lack of oxygen to the roots, when the leaves turn yellow, the roots rot and the plant dies.

WATERING SEEDLINGS

Seedlings at different stages require different watering. Freshly germinated seedlings will stay moist for longer than larger seedlings that take up water quickly. Be observant.

Lift your trays or pots – if they feel light, it's time to water.

In warm summer weather, established seedlings need a daily soak (sometimes twice a day if it is baking hot). In cooler weather, you may be able to leave two to three days between waterings.

Water from above with a watering can (with a rose) or the rose setting on a hose spray gun. Or make your own plastic watering bottle (see photograph above).

Pass the water over the tray. Allow it to soak in, then water again. Repeat until the tray feels heavy.

Act fast if seedlings wilt. Sink the tray in another tray or bowl of water and allow the seedlings to soak up water from below.

WATERING BEDS

Soils high in organic matter (achieved through adding compost) will hold onto moisture like a sponge, meaning less watering is needed.

The surface may look dry but push a finger 5cm (2in) into the soil; there may be moisture underneath.

Watering by hand with a watering can or hose is preferable to sprinklers, as plants have different needs and doing so is less wasteful. But sprinklers do save time!

Feeding

Your main priority for garden beds is to cultivate healthy soil, supporting your plants using compost – that means no extra feeding should be required. Pots are a different story and need regular feeds (see Feeding pots, page 36).

Making your own feed is a cheap, easy, deeply satisfying (if a little smelly) practice. Stinging nettles are high in nitrogen (N) and a good general tonic for leafy green crops. Comfrey (a leafy plant in the borage family) is rich in potassium (K) and other key nutrients. Both are a gardener's best friend, packed with nutrients to make liquid feeds. Both nettles and comfrey can irritate the skin, so wear gloves when handling them. Don't store either feed for long periods. Wormeries and bokashi bins also produce liquid feeds (see page 58).

COMFREY FEED

Comfrey feed encourages flowering and fruiting. If you don't have comfrey locally, grow your own (look for variety 'Bocking 14').

To make comfrey feed, use the method below for nettle feed, but add 1kg (2¼lb) leaves to 15 litres (4 gallons) water. Leave for four to six weeks, and don't dilute. Use the feed once the fruit sets (when the first tiny tomatoes develop or the first squash swells).

NETTLE FEED

1 Wearing gloves, gather 1kg (2¼lb) of young nettles without seeds or flowers (half a standard bucket).

2 Chop the leaves, then add 10 litres (2½ gallons) water (two watering cans). Weigh down the nettles and cover.

3 After two weeks, strain and bottle. Add the discarded nettle residue to the compost heap.

4 Dilute 1:10 with water to use as a feed.

Protecting your crops

↑ A fine insect mesh covering the container protects carrots from carrot fly.

Use physical barriers to protect crops from cold weather and damage from pests. See Resources, pages 220–1, for equipment.

HORTICULTURAL FLEECE

Protects plants from the cold and wind as you would with a warm blanket. Lay the fleece immediately on top of the plants and peg it down. They will push it up as they grow.

A huge support from early spring until temperatures warm, but it won't protect frost-tender plants completely. You must wait until after the last frost has passed to set those plants outside.

Different gauges are available – opt for 30gsm for longevity. It will become tatty over time but a few holes won't stop its effectiveness.

Can also be used as a pest barrier to keep flea beetle off radishes and delicate leafy brassicas, or to prevent carrot fly (although it is better to transition to insect mesh after the last frost).

Bubble wrap and upturned cardboard boxes can also be used to cover plants overnight but, unlike fleece, they need removing in the morning as they are not porous or breathable.

INSECT MESH

This breathable, fine fabric is laid over plants to prevent pest damage from flea beetle, carrot fly, birds, cabbage white butterflies and cabbage whitefly on brassicas. Weigh down the edges with stones or peg down as you would fleece (see above). For larger plants, construct a frame for the mesh with hoops or stakes (see page 74).

BUTTERFLY NETTING

Butterfly netting protects brassicas from cabbage white butterflies. Construct a cage using canes or stakes, put small pots on the cane tops, drape the netting over and peg down. For taller crops, like kale, the cage must be at least 1.4m (4½ft) high from the ground to the top of the stakes. Or metal garden hoops can be bought as a framework for netting (or insect mesh). Butterfly netting also doubles up as bird netting to deter hungry pigeons. For equipment, see Resources, pages 220–1.

Grow up

Using plant supports is a great way to maximize space, while also creating structure and beauty. There are plenty of ready-made options, from trellis and tepees to metal arches, or you can get creative with what you can source locally. Hazel makes great bean poles or canes for tomatoes, and squashes will climb up just about anything given a helping hand. If you're out walking, keep an eye out for fallen (unattached) branches to drag home and repurpose!

By growing plants up, you can utilize the bed space underneath for other edible plants. An understorey of herbs, edible flowers or salads around taller structures can shade the ground to lock in moisture, keep down the weeds and lure beneficial insects.

↑ Hazel tepees, with eight poles each, are used to support climbing French beans. See overleaf for how to make these. Look locally for coppiced hazel sources in the winter.

Key climbers in my Top 30

Squash (trailing varieties can be trained up)

Beans (French and runner)

Nasturtiums (trailing varieties)

Tomatoes (cordon types)

← Use sturdy branches as makeshift supports for climbing squashes. This winter squash is being trained out of its pot and up to the greenhouse, tied in place with jute twine in a figure-of-eight knot.

← An arch of runner beans forms a link between two raised bed edges, saving space and creating a beautiful focal point. See page 144 for planting instructions.

↓ A 'Delicata' squash plant reaches for the sky. Ready-made supports, such as this metal tower, are available to buy and can be reused year after year.

→ Winter squash, trailing nasturtiums and runner beans grow up this willow trellis, providing space for more crops to be planted in the rest of the bed.

Making a tepee step-by-step

Tepees are an effective and natural-looking way of training beans upwards. The principle is the same for in the ground as it is in pots – aim for a 45–60cm (1½–2ft) diameter tepee. I also wrap tepees with string as a support for trailing nasturtiums and climbing squashes (see 'Tromboncino', page 126).

What you'll need:

8 sticks, canes or poles (I prefer hazel), minimum 2m (6½ft) long

———

Large container (45–60cm/1½–2ft diameter)

———

Organic, peat-free multipurpose potting compost

———

String

———

Runner or French bean plants

———

1 Collect 8 sticks, canes or poles of roughly equal length. Fill a large container with potting compost. For best results, use 2.4m (8ft) sticks and a 60cm (2ft) diameter container. For smaller spaces, 2m (6½ft) sticks and a 45cm (1½ft) pot will work.

2 Position the sticks in the container 15–20cm (6–8in) apart, pushing down 20–30cm (8–12in) into the compost or as far as the pot will allow (for stability).

4 Plant the beans, one plant per stick for runners and two per stick for French beans. Leave the plants in cardboard if grown in the inner tubes of toilet rolls. Align the top of the rootballs with the soil surface and firm the soil gently around each plant. As the sticks will be close to the edge of the pot, plant the beans adjacent to the stick. Don't attempt to squash them in between the stick and the edge of the pot.

3 Gather the sticks together at the top with string, wrapping it around multiple times and securing with a tight knot.

5 Water well and gently guide the beans towards the sticks as they grow, tying them loosely with string to get them started if needs be.

Seed saving

Seed saving is one of the most powerful things you can do to take back control of your food. For millennia, our ancestors saved seeds, replanting them each year and developing varieties that were well adapted to their particular environment. This breeds more resilient crops. Saving your own seed also saves you money, and if you choose unusual heritage seeds, you are preventing rare varieties from being lost. In an often fragile-feeling world, it also offers a sense of security and makes the process of sowing seed even more enchanting.

To save seed, grow open-pollinated seed as opposed to F1.

POINTERS

* Save seed from your healthiest-looking plants.
* Ensure the seeds are fully dry before storing.
* Store in airtight containers in a cool, dry, dark place. I use jam jars.

F1 seeds

These hybrid varieties have been developed by plant breeders for favourable characteristics such as disease resistance, uniformity and yield – the last two being useful to commercial growers but not always so relevant to home growers. You cannot save seed from F1 hybrids. Seeds may germinate but will not offer any merits of the parent plant. They are not adaptable to evolving environments, which seems vital in a time of climate change. Around the world, subsistence farmers have become trapped in a cycle with certain seed

← Saved seed from the runner bean 'Scarlet Emperor', the French bean 'Cobra', nasturtiums and calendula.

↑ Removing seeds from the French bean 'Borlotto Lingua di Fuoco'.

companies, where they rely on buying new hybrid seed each year, while traditional varieties, grown for generations, are lost. This is not to bad-mouth all F1 hybrids, just to highlight the pitfalls. Your seed packet will tell you if it's an F1 variety.

Open-pollinated seeds

With open-pollinated seeds, pollination occurs by natural methods: by insects, birds, the wind or humans. Each generation of seed is similar to the previous and it adapts over time to its specific location. You can save seed from open-pollinated seed. But if you or a neighbour grow different varieties of the same vegetable, cross-pollination can occur. Specialist growers know how to prevent this – there is a lot of information out there (see Resources, pages 220–1). I see it as imperative to our future food security to support seed companies raising open-pollinated seed.

If you want an easy life, there are luckily a few vegetables that are self-fertile and it's very easy to save their seeds. If you're a beginner, I recommend starting with these first. Tomatoes, French beans, peas and lettuce are all self-pollinators, producing seed that will grow to be just like the parent plant, without the help of insects to transfer pollen between plants. See Resources, pages 220–1 for further seed-saving information.

Troubleshooting

An organic gardener must be crafty in tackling potential problems in the garden. Prevention is key when it comes to pests, diseases and weed pressure. These pages are designed to help you identify potential issues and ward them off where necessary.

↑ Check under the rims of pots for snails.

Pests

The word 'pest' is problematic, as these creatures all play their part in the food chain, and removing them leaves the predator hungry. Don't be trigger-happy eradicating pests – be patient and allow for natural checks and balances first.

Slugs & snails

Yes, they will eat your seedlings, but they also act as excellent composters eating decomposing vegetation, as well as providing food for song thrushes, hedgehogs, toads and ground beetles. Don't hate them – only a small number of the 40 slug species found in the UK are problematic to vegetable growers.

SYMPTOMS

Symptoms: A trail of slime, plus completely munched seedlings or large holes in bigger leaves.

PREVENTION

Keep your growing area tidy, removing potential hiding places like old plant pots, weeds and fallen leaves.

Create habitats for their predators with water sources, wood piles, long grass, hedgehog boxes, bird feeders, fruit trees and flowering plants.

Water in the morning – wet earth at night is more hospitable to slugs and snails.

SOLUTIONS

Go outside at night with a flashlight and pick them off by hand. If you don't want to kill them, deposit them at least 20m (65ft) from your garden, or they will return!

Place half an empty grapefruit skin, face down, in the garden to attract them. Leave overnight and remove in the morning.

Make exclusion barriers: cut a plastic bottle in half, remove the lid and use the top half as a mini cloche over seedlings at night. Remove in the morning, to avoid humidity, and replace again in the evening.

Wrap copper bands around pots (I've had mixed success with this).

Rough, sharp mulches like broken eggshells are thought to be uninviting for slugs and snails to crawl over, but I've never found them effective.

OTHER OPTIONS

Organic slug pellets: use them sparingly and as a last resort. NEVER buy pellets containing the poison metaldehyde, which is toxic to wildlife.

Wool pellets – a natural product (I've had mixed success with this).

For larger areas, use nematodes (naturally occurring microscopic parasitic worms), sold as a product that can be watered into damp soil. Avoid using near ponds.

← *A ladybird munching on aphids.*

APHIDS

Small sap-sucking insects – think greenfly and blackfly – distort new growth and transmit viruses.

———

Ants marching up plant stems are often a sign of aphids. Ants farm aphids, protecting them while harvesting the sticky honeydew they secrete.

———

Resist the urge to spray or squish – a range of insects and birds (especially blue tits) feed on aphids. If you're desperate, blast them off with a hose.

———

For windowsill plants, leave windows open to allow predatory insects inside. If problems spiral on windowsills, spritz aphids off with water in a spray bottle or hold the affected area under the tap.

———

It's easy to mistake aphid skins (small white casings) for whitefly (see Whitefly, opposite).

———

LETTUCE ROOT APHIDS

They colonize lettuce roots in midsummer, causing plants to wilt and die back, despite being watered. Affected plants need to be removed and composted.

———

Worse in dry conditions, so keep the soil moist.

———

It's possible to dig up lettuces, wash off the aphids and repot in fresh compost but it's only worth it if you have a small number of plants.

———

CABBAGE WHITE BUTTERFLIES

They eat leafy brassicas and nasturtiums, munching holes in their leaves.

———

The *large* white's caterpillars are black and yellow; the *small* white's are smaller, green and velvety.

———

Protect with insect mesh or butterfly netting (see page 71).

———

FLEA BEETLES

These tiny shiny beetles jump when the leaves are touched.

———

They create tiny pin-prick holes in the leaves of brassicas.

———

Cover plants or freshly sown seed with fine-gauge insect mesh or light-gauge fleece. They will soon find a way in if your fleece has holes or tears.

———

RED SPIDER MITES

Tiny sap-sucking mites.

———

Prevalent in greenhouses in hot, dry, crowded conditions.

———

Leaves appear mottled on the upper surface, then turn yellow and fall off; a silken web may be visible.

———

Keep humidity high, watering greenhouse floors in warm conditions.

———

FUNGUS GNATS (SCIARID FLIES)

Tiny flies seen running over the surface of compost on indoor and windowsill plants.

———

← A cabbage white butterfly.

← Rocket leaves with the pin-prick holes left by flea beetles.

Thrive in damp conditions, so don't overwater plants.

Cause little harm to established plants but the larvae can damage seedlings.

Use yellow sticky traps, or nematodes for bad infestations (both available online).

PIGEONS

They have a penchant for leafy brassicas!

Butterfly netting, as used to stop cabbage white butterflies, will also stop pigeons. For other birds, consider bird netting, but check daily to ensure no birds are trapped inside.

CARROT FLIES

Carrot fly larvae feed on the roots of carrots, creating brown tunnels.

The flies are attracted to the smell of bruised foliage.

Thin carrots on a still day with no wind, as the scent will not carry far. Evenings are best when the flies are less active.

Cover sown seed with fleece or insect mesh immediately, or construct a barrier 75cm (2½ft) high around the carrots using stakes and insect mesh. A top cover is not needed, as they are weak fliers and can't get up and over.

Cover containers with fleece or mesh. Growing in a tall container (minimum 75cm/2½ft in height) or placing pots on a table can outwit carrot fly, as can surrounding carrots with chives (the smell confuses them).

LEAF MINERS

Larvae create pale yellow lesions on leaves.

Can affect beetroot, chard and spinach. I eat the leaves regardless if the damage isn't bad. Otherwise dispose of affected leaves to compost.

WHITEFLY

Tiny sap-feeding insect, mainly affecting greenhouse crops and windowsill plants.

Clouds of winged insects take flight when the plant is disturbed.

Indoor tomatoes are susceptible. Grow with French marigolds and basil to confuse the pest, and leave doors open to welcome in beneficial predatory insects.

For windowsills, see Aphids (opposite) or use sticky traps (see Fungus gnats, opposite).

CATS

Enjoy using beds as litter trays.

Net your beds or lay sharp twigs or foliage, such as holly, between plants.

Pests:
Top tips

↑ Parsley in flower in its second year is a great lure for hoverflies.

Pests have certain seasons or conditions when they are most prevalent. As a gardener, paying attention to sowing times is key – crops sown at the wrong time of year are vulnerable. (See Top 30 spotlights, from page 110, for individual sowing times.)

Consider companion planting, which is growing certain plants that are mutually beneficial next to each other or at the ends of beds. Companion planting can be used to attract beneficial insects, repel pests, create trap crops (see below) and design polycultures (see Looking good, page 38).

Attracting beneficial insects

Allowing all the herbs in my Top 30 to flower will attract a range of beneficial insects, as well as providing edible flowers.

Allow parsley to flower in its second year, to attract hoverflies.

Grow calendula to attract lacewings.

Apple blossom provides early forage.

Don't be hasty to mow the flowers from your lawn, and leave longer patches of grass.

Allow nettles to flourish (within reason) – to attract ladybirds.

See also Beneficial insects, page 61.

REPELLING INSECT PESTS

French marigolds may repel whitefly with the smell of their foliage.

Plants in the onion family, such as chives, can repel carrot fly.

TRAP CROPS

Sow sacrificial crops to draw pests away from your plants, although the counter argument says this just builds numbers!

Nasturtiums attract cabbage white butterflies and blackfly, potentially luring them away from your brassicas.

Diseases

↓ Although outdoor tomatoes are more susceptible to blight, this fungal disease can still affect indoor crops. Ensure there is adequate ventilation.

Like us, plants succumb to disease. Creating robust ecosystems with mixed plantings and healthy soil buffers your plants against disease, much like bolstering your own immune system. Diseases still strike but may be less rampant. Only common diseases that affect the plants in this book are listed here.

BLIGHT, LATE

Affects tomatoes, potatoes.

It's a fungal disease that causes brown patches on the leaves and blackening stems, leading to the plant rotting and collapsing.

Spores multiply in warm, humid conditions and wet summers.

Outdoor crops are the worst affected but it can still strike in greenhouses.

I focus on early potatoes, which are cropped before the threat arrives. Blight-resistant potato varieties are available.

Ensure the airflow is good around plants and avoid getting water on foliage.

Avoid growing tomatoes and potatoes next to each other, as blight can quickly spread between them.

Blighted plants can be buried in your compost – there's no need to burn them.

DAMPING OFF

Affects all seedlings.

Fungal disease that causes greenhouse seedlings to collapse. White fungal growth is spotted. Lack of airflow and damp conditions make it worse.

Keep seedlings well ventilated; don't sow too thickly; take care not to overwater.

BLOSSOM END ROT

Affects tomatoes.

Bottom of the fruit becomes brown/black and sunken, caused by a lack of calcium in the fruits due to erratic watering.

Water consistently; keep the soil/compost moist.

→ White powdery mildew as seen on the leaves of this courgette plant.

POWDERY MILDEW

Affects courgettes, apples.

Fungal disease that creates a white, powdery coating on the leaves and stems of plants.

Worsens during dry conditions.

A common problem when growing courgettes. Keep plants well watered and cut out badly affected leaves.

If apple leaves are affected, prune out infected shoots and buds in winter. In spring, prune infected leaves and shoots into a bag and compost them.

DOWNY MILDEW

Affects lettuce.

Fungal disease that occurs most in wet summers.

Discoloured patches appear on the leaf surface and white/grey mould underneath.

Remove affected leaves.

Regularly picking lettuce leaves helps.

CLUBROOT

Affects kale and other brassicas.

Plants wilt in dry weather, despite being watered.

Roots become distorted and the plant stunted and sickly.

The best way to avoid it is to rotate brassica crops, that is, don't grow brassicas in the same bed year on year (see Rotations, opposite).

Diseases: Top tips

* Maintain healthy soil: applying good compost will increase the resilience of plants.
* Practise good husbandry: keep tools clean and the growing area tidy and weed free.
* Consider disease-resistant varieties, such as blight-resistant potatoes.
* Avoid growing the same family of vegetables (see right) in the same place year on year (see also Rotations, below).

Rotations

Rotating what you grow can prevent soil-borne diseases. The standard rotation is four years before planting an area again with the same family. Divide your plot into four sections, list the crops in their families (see chart) and make a plan. You may need to subdivide beds to include more families.

Rotate what you grow in your pots, too.

If you have a small space with only a few beds, this is tough and can dictate what you grow, rather than what you *want* to grow. With annual applications of good compost, a few years between plants is better than nothing.

Within one season, aim to avoid repetition of the same family where possible. Cucurbits, legumes and lettuces don't need a long rotation –

just mix them up where you can. Try to keep a longer gap between potatoes and brassicas. Luckily, kale is a less problematic brassica, so there's no cause for concern if you can't leave a four-year gap, and salad leaf brassicas and radish are in the ground for a short time, so don't need to be treated with as much caution. Consider rotating potatoes between bags and beds if necessary.

Always keep notes of what you planted where previously.

VEGETABLE & HERB FAMILIES

I've included plants not mentioned in this book as it's interesting to see the full picture.

Family	Vegetables
Allium	Chives, garlic, leek, onion, spring onion, shallot
Amaranth	Beetroot, chard, leaf beet, spinach
Brassicas	Broccoli, Brussels sprouts, cabbage, cauliflower, kale, kohlrabi, land cress, Asian greens, radish, rocket, swede, turnip
Cucurbit	Courgette, cucumber, melon, squash
Legume	Broad bean, French bean, runner bean, pea
Daisy	Artichokes, chicory, endive, lettuce
Mint	Basil, marjoram, mint, rosemary, sage, thyme
Polygonaceae	Rhubarb, sorrel
Solanum	Aubergine, chilli, pepper, potato, tomato
Umbellifer	Carrot, celery, celeriac, chervil, coriander, dill, fennel, parsley, parsnip

Weeds

↑ The delicate leaves of oxalis look beautiful in salads.

Like pests, don't always view weeds as the enemy. Many are beautiful plants that support wildlife and have important edible and medicinal roles to play. I will never fail to be cheered by the dandelions in my lawn, and allow the edible weeds listed below a place at the edges of my plot.

* Weeds amid your vegetables can be problematic, so be observant and remove them before they set seed. Pluck out with your fingers, a hand fork or hoe off (on a dry day). If you're confused between weeds and your seedlings, allow the second set of leaves to come through and compare them to the seed you've sown.

* The less you disturb the soil by digging, the fewer weed seeds you'll throw to the surface. Practice no-dig methods (see page 44) mulching beds with 3–5cm (1–2in) of garden compost in winter.

* Cardboard or black polythene is useful if you want to clear weeds from a patch of ground. If laid down for around three months, they exclude light, killing annual weeds and weakening perennial ones. Perennial weeds should be removed with a hand fork before creating beds. Biodegradable mulch sheets are also available that you can plant straight through.

EDIBLE WEEDS

Of the so-called weeds shown opposite, the young leaves of hairy bittercress, chickweed, oxalis and dandelion (leaves and flower petals) are all delicious in spring salads. Oxalis brings the sour, dandelion the bitter, bittercress the peppery punch and chickweed balances these flavours with delicate, grassy notes. The young spring leaves of ground elder are also good in soups and salads, and fat hen leaves can be cooked like spinach. If you are interested in eating wild plants, always consult a good foraging book for proper identification and possible cautions (see Resources, pages 220–1).

Note: Don't consume large quantities of oxalis or fat hen due to their oxalic acid content which is toxic in excessive amounts. Use sparingly, avoid giving to children or if pregnant or breastfeeding.

Common annual weeds

1 Hairy bittercress

2 Chickweed

3 Fat hen

4 Groundsel

5 Shepherd's purse

6 Speedwell

Common perennial weeds

7 Bindweed

8 Dandelion

9 Dock

10 Ground elder

11 Mare's tail

12 Oxalis

13 Stinging nettle

Recipe
Nettles two ways

IN DEPTH:
STINGING NETTLE

Nutritional powerhouses with medicinal value, nettles are also supportive of more than 40 insect species, and can provide a nitrogen-rich feed for other plants.

Nettles are rich in vitamins C and A, as well as a range of minerals. They are used in herbal medicine as an all-round tonic; the seeds, roots and leaves can be used for varying purposes. The simplest way to harness the good stuff is to make nettle tea.

Nettles are recognizable but be sure to choose them well. Avoid picking from polluted roadsides or field margins that may have been sprayed. Look for new, fresh shoots. Take the top two to three sets of leaves before flowering occurs. Cut your patch down in late spring to encourage new summer growth. Remember that nettles sting. Always wear gloves when handling.

As with all regular herb consumption, consult a medical herbalist if you are pregnant, breastfeeding or have underlying health issues. Do not give to children under the age of two years; particular care should be taken for children over the age of two years.

NETTLE TEA Pick 2–3 sprigs of fresh nettle tops (the first 2–3 sets of leaves with stems) per person – pick in spring when nettles are young and fresh, or dry in spring for use year-round. Place in a teapot, fill with hot water and pop the lid on – the lid prevents volatile oils escaping and retains the nettle's beneficial properties. Alternatively, use a mug with a saucer on top. Allow to steep for 5–10 minutes, depending on how strong you like your tea, before drinking. One or two cups daily is a good amount.

NETTLE SOUP This is hands-down my favourite soup. After the long malaise of winter, it sets you up for the season ahead. Remember to wear gloves while prepping.

Wash and drain the nettles. Heat 50g (1¾oz) of butter (or 2 tbsp olive oil) in a saucepan and add 1 chopped onion, 2 chopped garlic cloves and 1 diced carrot and cook until softened. Add 1 litre (1¾ pints) vegetable or chicken stock, 1 large peeled and chopped potato and bring to the boil. Cook until soft (10-–15 minutes), then add 2 large handfuls of nettle tops. Cook for a further 2 minutes. Blitz with a hand blender or in a blender. Season to taste with salt and pepper. Spoon into bowls. Finish with a drizzle of olive oil.

→ Homemade nettle tea.

Year-round planner

This is a quick reference guide to what you should be doing each month, particularly when it comes to sowing seed. For details of each crop, see Top 30 spotlights (from page 110)

The following pages include two separate seed sowing calendars – one is for indoor sowing, where plants are started in modules, seed trays or pots, appropriate for people who have some indoor space where they can start their seeds, such as a windowsill or greenhouse.

Raise plants indoors first where possible, but if you have no space to do this, the second chart shows when crops can be sown directly outside. You can sow straight into your pots or beds, or you can still sow into modules at these times. If you are buying module or nursery-grown plants, use the direct sowing calendar as a guide to when it is safe to plant these outside.

The rest of the planner shows key monthly tasks and planting times for key crops.

← Sowing beetroot seed, three seeds per module.

KEY TASKS – A MONTH-BY-MONTH GUIDE

These are the monthly garden tasks and planting times for key plants in my Top 30.

MONTH	ACTIVITY
January/ February	Have some down time. First sowings start in February.
	If you haven't already done so, make a plan for the year ahead, order seeds and plants.
	Tidy indoor growing spaces. Organize tools, equipment and pots.
	If you haven't spread compost on beds or pots in autumn, do it now (see September).
	Chit seed potatoes as soon as they arrive.
	Force early varieties of rhubarb in January.
	Prune blueberries in late February to early March (not required if plants are under two years old). New plants can be planted now, if not done so in autumn.
	Plant bare-root apple trees if you haven't done so in autumn.
	Winter-prune apples.
	Plant rhubarb crowns until late February.
March	Weeding. Use your hoe to remove any emerging weed seeds. Wait for a dry day as hoeing in wet soil damages its structure. Some weeds make delicious additions to spring salads (see Edible weeds, page 86).
	Plant first early potatoes (from mid- to late March).
	Plant blueberries and bare-root apples if not already done.
	Plant pot-grown or bare-root strawberry runners if not done so in autumn.
	Overwintered salad leaves, such as claytonia, corn salad, land cress and spinach, will be coming to life again.
April	General weeding.
	Feeding pots with liquid feed can start (see page 36).
	Plant second early potatoes (early to mid-April) and maincrop (mid- to late April).

MONTH	ACTIVITY
April cont'd	Earth up first early potatoes.
	Plant strawberries if not done so in autumn. Pot-grown, bare-root and cold-stored runners can go in this month.
	Take cuttings from rose geranium and mint to build up stock (see Mint cuttings, page 173, and Rose geranium, page 208).
	When the soil warms, plant out potted herbs – chives, mint, parsley, rosemary, sage, tarragon and thyme – into pots or beds. Note: lemon verbena, rose geranium and basil can only be planted after all danger of frost has passed, after mid-May.
May	Stay on top of weeding and watering.
	Earth up potatoes.
	Clear any overwintered salad.
	Protect apple blossom and blueberry flowers from late frost with fleece.
	Thin carrots and pinch out tomatoes.
	Wait until after the last frosts to plant out tomatoes (indoors and out), courgettes, winter squashes, basil, French marigolds, lemon verbena and rose geranium.
	Plant cold-stored strawberry runners.
	Harvests are less abundant this month – it's still the 'hungry gap'.
June	Weeding and watering.
	Plant French and runner beans after the last frost.
	Continue to earth up maincrop potatoes.
	Pinch out and tie in tomatoes to supports.
	Tie in climbing squashes to supports.
	Thin carrots.
	Harvests will be picking up, with first early potatoes, early carrots, first strawberries, beetroot, salads, radish and fresh herbs abundant.

MONTH	ACTIVITY
July	Watering.
	Pinch out and tie in tomatoes to supports.
	Tie in climbing squashes to supports.
	Thin carrots.
	Harvests become more abundant through to September.
	Keep deadheading flowers.
	Summer-prune apples (from mid-July to early August).
August	Weeding and watering.
	Clear beds and pots to make way for winter plantings in September.
	Spread compost (before any overwintering crops go in). No-dig systems require a top-up of 3–5cm (1–2in) of your chosen compost.
	Pinch out and tie in tomatoes to supports.
	Keep an eye out for blight on tomatoes and potatoes (see Diseases, page 83).
	Thin carrots.
	Tie in climbing squashes to supports.
	Many of the winter salads are sown this month.
	Plant pot-grown or bare-root strawberry runners.
September	Clear plants and add compost to any areas that will be bare over winter. No-dig systems require a top-up of 3–5cm (1–2in) of your chosen compost.
	Plant pot-grown or bare-root strawberry runners.
	September is a bountiful month when summer and autumn crops collide. Potentially all crops in my Top 30 are available, other than rhubarb and winter squash.
	Feeding pots with liquid feed can stop for winter, unless for autumn/winter crops in pots (see page 36).
	Collet dried seedheads of plants you're saving, for sowing next year.

MONTH	ACTIVITY
October	Collect dried seedheads of plants you're planning to sow next year.
	Clear plants and add compost (see September).
	Plant rhubarb crowns until February.
	It's still possible to plant pot-grown or bare-root strawberry runners, although August/September is better.
	No more sowings inside or out for Top 30 plants until next year.
	Bring lemon verbena and rose geranium indoors, which can both be killed by frost (see Herb spotlights, pages 170, 208, for more information) and protect tarragon (see page 182).
	Protect young sage, rosemary and thyme plants with fleece on frosty nights.
	In colder areas, before the first frosts, protect potted blueberries by raising pots off the ground with bricks or insulating with bubble wrap.
November	Clear plants and add compost (see September).
	Plan crops and order seeds for next year.
	Plant bare-root apples from now until March.
	Prune apples from November to March.
	Plant rhubarb crowns from November to late February.
	Plant blueberries from November to March (or in spring/summer if necessary).
December	As for November. Time to put your feet up!

SOWING CALENDAR FOR PLANTS IN MY TOP 30 – INDOOR SOWING

If you have no space to raise plants indoors, use the Direct Sowing (Outdoors) calendar. Some seeds require warmth – see The Top 30, page 110.

MONTH	CROP	NOTES
January		
February	Radish and pea shoots in multi-sown modules (all from mid Feb)	
	Tomatoes (from late-Feb to mid-March)	For greenhouse/indoor tomatoes
	Alpine strawberries, spinach and lettuce (all from mid-Feb)	
March	Radish and pea shoots in multi-sown modules	
	Tomatoes (before mid-March)	For tomatoes that will be grown indoors/greenhouse
	Tomatoes (March to early April)	For tomatoes that will be grown outdoors
	Beetroot	Use variety 'Boltardy' in March
	Spinach, lettuce, chives, parsley, French sorrel, calendula, French marigold	
	Viola	For spring/summer flowers
April	Radish in multi-sown modules	
	Tomatoes (early April only)	For tomatoes that will be grown outdoors
	Courgette (mid- to late April)	Preferred date
	Winter squash (mid-April)	Preferred date
	Lettuce, spinach, beetroot, calendula, French marigold, chard, Kale, New Zealand spinach (mid-April), French sorrel, basil, nasturtium	
May	Beetroot, radish in multi-sown modules, calendula, French marigold, chard, courgette (until early June), winter squash (early May only), lettuce, kale, French sorrel, basil, nasturtium, French and runner beans (from mid-May to mid-June), summer purslane	

MONTH	CROP	NOTES
June	Beetroot, radish in multi-sown modules, chard, courgette (early June only), lettuce, kale, French sorrel, basil, nasturtium, French and runner beans (until mid-June), summer purslane	
	Viola	For autumn/winter flowers
July	Beetroot (early July only), radish in multi-sown modules, chard, lettuce, summer purslane (early July only), kale (early July only)	
	Viola	For autumn/winter flowers
	Chervil (late July to early August), Spinach (late July to mid-August)	
August	Radish in multi-sown modules	
	Calendula	Overwinter for early flowering
	Lettuce	Winter varieties
	Rocket, land cress, claytonia, chicory leaves (early August only)	
	Spinach (until mid-August), corn salad (end August), Asian leaves	
September	Calendula	Overwinter for early flowering
	Viola	Overwinter for early flowering
	Asian leaves	
	Lettuce (early September only)	Winter varieties
October		
November		
December		

Note:
• If growing salads in a greenhouse over winter, sow in early September.
• Microgreens can be sown year-round, see page 26.

SOWING CALENDAR FOR PLANTS IN MY TOP 30 – DIRECT SOWING (OUTDOORS)

MONTH	CROP	NOTES
January		
February		
March	Lettuce, spinach, pea shoots, parsley, radish, first early potatoes (from mid- to late March)	
	Carrot (late March)	Early varieties
April	Second early potatoes (early to mid-April)	Can also be sown in March
	Main crop potatoes (mid- to late April)	
	Carrots	Early varieties
	Lettuce, spinach, pea shoots, beetroot, parsley, chard, kale, radish, French sorrel, calendula	
May	Lettuce, beetroot, carrot, chard, kale, radish, French sorrel, calendula, summer purslane, French and runner beans (late May), courgette (late May), winter squash (mid-late May), nasturtium (mid-late May), French marigold (mid-late May)	
June	Lettuce, beetroot, carrot, chard, kale, radish, French sorrel, French and runner beans (until mid-June), courgette (early June only), nasturtium, summer purslane	
July	Lettuce, chard, radish	
	Beetroot, kale, summer purslane (all early July)	
	Carrot (by mid-July), chervil, spinach, rocket (all late July)	
	Chicory leaves (late July)	For baby leaves
August	Lettuce, radish, chervil, rocket, land cress, claytonia (all early August), corn salad (mid-August), spinach (by mid-August), Asian leaves	
	Chicory leaves (early August)	For baby leaves
	Calendula	Overwinter plants for earlier spring flowers

MONTH	CROP	NOTES
September	Calendula	Overwinter plants for earlier spring flowers
	Asian leaves	
October		
November		
December		

↑ Tying in winter squash to its support.

Crop plan for two raised beds

This is a blueprint for two raised beds (1.2 × 2.4m/4 × 8ft) that will provide you with continuous harvests nearly all year round. The plan crops well for my garden in the southeast of England. It assumes the soil will be starting to warm by mid-March.

↑ These two compact raised beds have been designed for continuous harvests.

The beds

↑ Once constructed, the raised beds can be planted straightaway.

These beds are designed as no dig, meaning you can build straight onto lawns, existing beds or even concrete without turning the soil beneath. See Raised beds, page 40 onwards, before starting.

Build beds in your sunniest spot, sheltered from the wind. It doesn't matter which is bed 1 and which is bed 2. Depending on their orientation (see page 45), tepees may cast a little shade, but salad crops won't complain.

Ensure the internal measurements are 1.2m (4ft) and 2.4m (8ft) to follow the plan. A width of 1.2m (4ft) enables you to reach the centre from both sides, without having to walk on it, potentially compacting the soil. Having said that, no-dig raised beds are more robust, as the soil is protected by a decent layer of compost. Although garden railway sleepers look good, they are chunky and will limit the internal bed measurements for this plan. For other options for wooden sides, see pages 41–2.

What you'll need:

1½ bulk bags of planting medium to fill the beds (see Filling beds, page 45)

Seed and potting compost

2 module trays, minimum 60 cells each (see page 14)

16 sticks or canes, to make 2 tepees

Trellis for winter squash, measuring 1.2m (4ft) wide × 1.1m (3½ft) high. The height measurement is loose – it can be a little taller but no shorter than 1m (39in). Buy ready-made trellis, securing it to sturdy upright stakes banged into the soil below (stakes can also be screwed into the side of the bed for security), or screw together wood offcuts to make your own rustic trellis (see photo opposite).

Horticultural fleece (enough to cover both beds)

Insect mesh (optional – fleece can be used instead, but mesh is best)

Butterfly netting, plus canes or hoops for framework (see page 71)

Cold frame or mini-greenhouse (optional, but will make life easier in spring, preventing windowsill legginess)

← One of the raised beds in early summer, showing the homemade hazel screen for supporting the winter squash.

→ You will need two module trays (with a minimum of 60 cells each) to follow the plan.

* Winter radish and lettuce will have been harvested.
* Potatoes can be planted alongside chard and spinach – keep cropping salads until potatoes need more light, then remove the salads.
* You will only fit in one row of February-sown radish.
* Once carrots need more light/ space in April, remove spinach and chicory. The same goes for rocket, mustard, land cress and claytonia – once beetroot plugs need the space, remove plants. Beware of slugs lurking under current foliage that may munch new seedlings – keep overwintered plants well picked and tidy.
* Fleece still needs to be laid over new sowings/plantings, so cover the whole bed with fleece for ease.
* If you feel overwintered plants are still giving when it is time to remove them, pick hard and try potting up a few. They may well bolt but that could give you some pretty flowers.

POINTERS

* Use the bed plans and charts together. The bed plan provides measurements, the chart detailed sowing information.
* Be sure to follow the sowing dates. In very cold springs, you may need to start a little later. Spring sowings can catch up, but summer sowings must be more precise – be aware that you cannot sow courgettes later than early June or winter squash past May, and winter salad sowing dates should not be any later than stated.
* Sowings should be done into module trays, unless stated as 'direct sown'. For how to sow a module tray, see page 62.
* Always note the amount of seedlings per module listed in the chart as this is the number of seedings you need when planting out. You can over-sow to ensure germination, but make sure you thin to the number listed before planting.
* See Top 30 spotlights from page 110 for in-depth growing advice, harvesting and suggested varieties.

ROTATIONS

This plan can be rotated between the two beds year on year. In year 2, simply switch beds, growing crops from bed 1 in bed 2 and vice versa. In the second year, you'll have overwintered salads in bed 2 in spring. Continue to follow the crop plan:

Crop plan: Spring

↑ Multi-sown beetroot seedlings.

Start seedlings in the warmth. Windowsills, conservatories and greenhouses can all be put to good use. See Windowsill tips & tricks, page 23, and Greenhouses, pages 18–19.

POINTERS

* Wait until mid-February to start sowing (no earlier).
* Direct sowings and plantings in spring must be covered with fleece. Also use it to protect later radish sowings from flea beetle.
* Make all February sowings in one module tray, reserving the other for March.

BED 1 (YEAR 1)

Choose early carrots, 'Boltardy' beetroot and first early potatoes, as they need to be harvested in early June to make way for summer crops. For a wider potato selection, consider planting in bags too. For varieties, see Top 30 spotlights, page 110.

To prevent windowsill legginess, after a few weeks of growth, ideally move seedlings to a cold frame (see pages 18–19) or an unheated greenhouse before planting out. Offer extra protection of fleece at night.

The first sowing of radish is for planting between potatoes (plant at the same time as potatoes). They grow fast and will be harvested before potatoes are established.

Note: carrots are sown direct into drills in the bed, not into modules first (see page 68).

BED 2 (YEAR 1)

Lettuce is picked from around the base, not as whole heads (see Salad leaves, page 146). 'Little Gem' lettuces are picked as whole heads.

Pick pea shoots continuously from April to early June (see page 150).

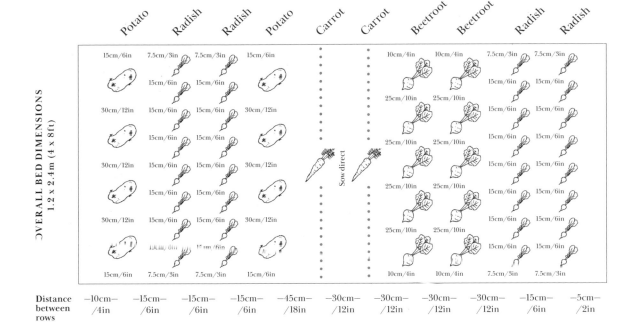

Crop	Sow indoors	Number of modules	Seedlings per module	Plant out	Sow direct outdoors	Harvest	Notes
Potato, first early		4 tubers			March (mid)	June	
Radish	February (late)	8	4	March (mid)		April	
Radish	February (late)	8	4	March (mid)		April	
Potato, first early		4 tubers			March (mid)	June	
Carrot, early					March (late)	June	Approximately 2 seeds per 1cm/¼in. After 1 month thin to 1 seed per 1cm/¼in.
Carrot, early					March (late)	June	As above.
Beetroot 'Boltardy'	March (early)	5	4	April (early)		June	
Beetroot 'Boltardy'	March (early)	5	4	April (early)		June	
Radish	March (mid)	8	4	April (early)		April	
Radish	April (early)	8	4	April (mid)		May	

Planting layout labels (left to right): Parsley · Lettuce · Lettuce · Little Gem · Little Gem · Radish · Pea shoots · Pea shoots · Spinach · Spinach

OVERALL BED DIMENSIONS 1.2 x 2.4m (4 x 8ft)

Distance between rows	—10cm—/4in	—22cm—/8½in	—22cm—/8½in	—22cm—/8½in	—22cm—/8½in	—22cm—/8½in	—25cm—/10in	—25cm—/10in	—25cm—/10in	—25cm—/10in	—20cm—/8in

Crop	Sow indoors	Number of modules	Seedlings per module	Plant out	Sow direct outdoors	Harvest	Notes
Parsley	March	8	1	April		May/June/July	
Lettuce	Feb (mid/late)	6	1	April (early)		May to July	Harvest leaves from around the base, not whole heads.
Lettuce	Feb (mid/late)	6	1	April (early)		May to July	As above.
Little Gem	Feb (mid/late)	6	1	April (early)		May/June	Harvest as whole heads.
Little Gem	Feb (mid/late)	6	1	April (early)		May/June	As above.
Radish	March (end)	8	4	April (mid)		April/May	
Peashoots	Feb (mid)	5	4	March (mid)		April to June	
Peashoots	Feb (mid)	5	4	March (mid)		April to June	
Spinach, early	Feb (mid)	5	3	March (mid)		April to June	
Spinach, early	Feb (mid)	5	3	March (mid)		April to June	

Crop plan: Summer

As spring crops are cleared, summer crops take their place. Remember: beans, squash, courgettes, tomatoes and nasturtiums are all frost tender, so don't plant them out until the stated dates.

BED 1 (YEAR 1)

Put up trellis and tepees before planting anything (see Beans, pages 142–3).

Ensure you start beans, courgettes and winter squash in pots, not modules (9cm/3½in pots or equivalent).

Tomatoes need a long growing season, so must be started at the date stated, but will need potting into bigger pots to keep them going. If winter squash or other modules look in need of a pot size up before spring crops are finished, then pot those on too.

Select an early bush tomato variety that won't need staking (see Tomatoes, page 154).

If you have space to put your tomatoes in pots instead of in raised beds, there is the option to replace the tomatoes with another courgette plant.

Pick some beans fresh, but leave a picking on plants at the end of the season for dried beans in winter, and to save the seed.

Keep tying squashes onto trellis so that they grow up and don't swamp other plants.

Kale needs butterfly netting – I've left a gap around the outside of plants to fit this in.

BED 2 (YEAR 1)

Parsley remains in place from its spring planting.

Summer purslane, carrot and radish are sown direct into the raised bed.

→ Runner bean plants grown in toilet roll tubes.

Carrots and radish need covering with fléece or insect mesh on sowing, to protect from carrot fly and flea beetle. This can be laid over rows and pegged down.

BED 1: SUMMER

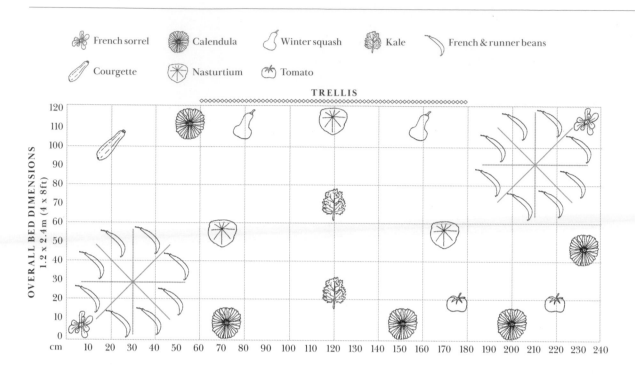

Legend:
- French sorrel
- Calendula
- Winter squash
- Kale
- French & runner beans
- Courgette
- Nasturtium
- Tomato

TRELLIS

OVERALL BED DIMENSIONS 1.2 x 2.4m (4 x 8ft)

Crop	Sow indoors	Number of modules	Seedlings per module	Plant out	Sow direct outdoors	Harvest	Notes
Beans, climbing French	May (late)	8 pots	2	June		Aug to Oct	
Beans, runner	May (late)	8 pots	1	June		Aug to Oct	
Calendula	May (mid)	5	1	June		July onwards	
Courgette	May (mid)	1 pot	1	June		July to Sept	If you have space to grow tomatoes in pots, you could grow 2 courgettes instead.
Kale	May (late)	2	1	June		July onwards	
Nasturtium	May (mid)	3	1	June		July to Oct	
French sorrel	May (mid)	2	3	June		June/July onwards	
Winter squash	May (mid)	2 pots	1	June		Oct	
Tomato	April (early)	2	1	June		July to Sept	

BED 2: SUMMER

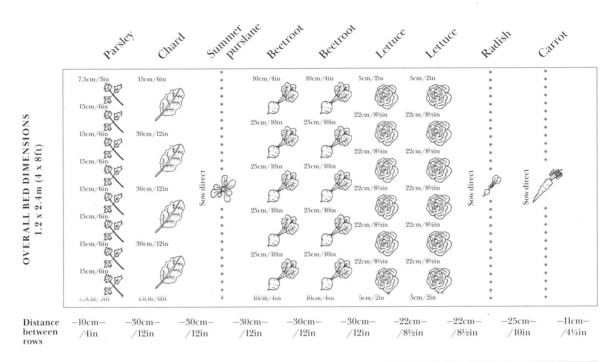

OVERALL BED DIMENSIONS
1.2 x 2.4m (4 x 8ft)

	Parsley	Chard	Summer purslane	Beetroot	Beetroot	Lettuce	Lettuce	Radish	Carrot
Distance between rows	—10cm—/4in	—30cm—/12in	—30cm—/12in	—30cm—/12in	—30cm—/12in	—30cm—/12in	—22cm—/8½in	—22cm—/8½in	—25cm—/10in	—11cm—/4¼in

Crop	Sow indoors	Number of modules	Seedlings per module	Plant out	Sow direct outdoors	Harvest	Notes
Parsley							Still in place from April planting.
Chard	June (early)	4	2	July		Aug onwards	
Summer purslane					July	Aug/Sept	Thin to 1 seedling per 10cm (4in).
Beetroot	April (late)	5	4	May (late)		July	
Beetroot	April (late)	5	4	May (late)		July	
Lettuce	June (early)	6	1	July		July to Sept	
Lettuce	June (early)	6	1	July		July to Sept	
Radish					June	July/Aug	Thin to 1 seedling per 3cm (1¼in).
Carrot					June	Aug/Sept	Approximately 2 seeds per 1cm/¼in. After 1 month thin to 1 seedling per 1cm/¼in.

Crop plan: Autumn/Winter

You will be left with one bed with just kale and sorrel in to overwinter. The other will have overwintering salads.

POINTERS

* Both beds will need composting once the summer crops are cleared, before any autumn plantings. This may have to happen a row at a time as plants are cleared. Spread an annual top-up of 3–5cm (1–2in). There's no need to dig it in – just leave on the surface and worms will do the hard work.
* Don't sow winter crops late, as they may not establish enough before winter.
* Although less active in autumn when leaves are picked, flea beetle can still affect August-sown seedlings of rocket, land cress, Asian greens and winter radish. Lay fleece or insect mesh over the entire bed to stop any attacks as soon as you've sown or planted. You can remove the fleece in October, and only use in really cold snaps, as it can lower light levels.
* Chervil (sown late July/early August) could be swapped with winter salads or sown direct in a pot. And sow parsley in a pot in July for continued windowsill harvests over winter. It's also worth digging up and repotting one of the parsley plants in your raised bed, before you clear plants to make way for winter radish. Parsley is biennial and will flower the following year. This looks beautiful and will be a real treat for hoverflies.

BED 1 (YEAR 1)

Winter squash and dried beans can be harvested from September or October.

———

Courgettes, nasturtiums and tomatoes will be killed by first frosts if they have not already been removed.

———

Leave in kale for slim winter pickings.

———

Leave in sorrel and protect with fleece in cold weather. It will give spring leaves.

———

Calendula can offer blooms into early winter, but must be cleared before March plantings.

———

→ The winter radish 'Rosa' and the daikon radish 'Minowase'.

BED 2 (YEAR 1)

Grow a mix of winter radish varieties (see Radish, page 138).

If lettuce is still going strong when you need to plant winter salad, interplant modules between lettuce and keep picking it. As soon as the interplanted winter salads need more space, remove the lettuce.

Winter radish is cropped in autumn. Lettuce will finish in early autumn. The remaining salad leaves will offer autumn and early winter pickings, then romp away in early spring.

Mustard and rocket will flower in late spring – the flowers are peppery, delicious and a feast for pollinators.

← Spinach, sown late-July to mid-August, for overwintering.

BED 1: AUTUMN/WINTER

 French sorrel   Calendula   Winter squash   Kale French & runner beans

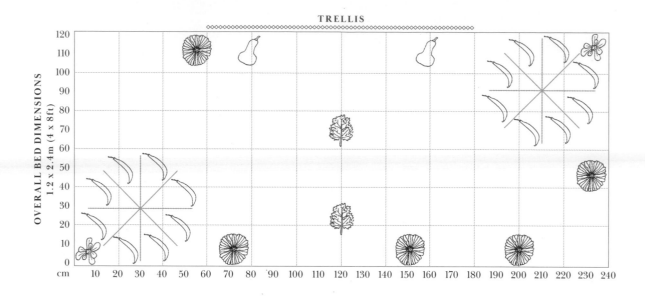

Crop	Sow indoors	Number of modules	Seedlings per module	Plant out	Sow direct outdoors	Harvest	Notes
Beans, climbing French						Sept/Oct	Still in place from June planting – in Sept/Oct save seed for next year and harvest dried beans to eat.
Beans, runner						Sept/Oct	Still in place from June planting – in Sept/Oct save seed for next year and harvest dried beans to eat.
Calendula						into early winter	Still in place from June planting.
Kale						will overwinter	Still in place from June planting.
French sorrel						will overwinter	Still in place from June planting.
Winter squash						October	Still in place from June planting.

BED 2: AUTUMN/WINTER

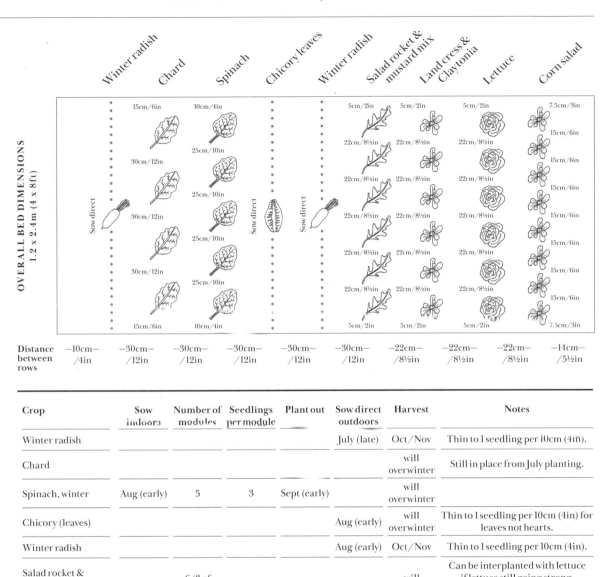

Crop	Sow indoors	Number of modules	Seedlings per module	Plant out	Sow direct outdoors	Harvest	Notes
Winter radish					July (late)	Oct/Nov	Thin to 1 seedling per 10cm (4in).
Chard						will overwinter	Still in place from July planting.
Spinach, winter	Aug (early)	5	3	Sept (early)		will overwinter	
Chicory (leaves)					Aug (early)	will overwinter	Thin to 1 seedling per 10cm (4in) for leaves not hearts.
Winter radish					Aug (early)	Oct/Nov	Thin to 1 seedling per 10cm (4in).
Salad rocket & Mustard/Asian leaf mix	Aug (late)	6 (3 of each)	3	Sept		will overwinter	Can be interplanted with lettuce if lettuce still going strong. Remove lettuce once other leaves establish.
Land cress & Claytonia	Aug (early)	6 (3 of each)	1	Sept		will overwinter	As above.
Lettuce	July (mid)	6	1	Aug		will overwinter	
Corn salad	Aug (late)	8	1	Sept (late)		will overwinter	

The top 30

This chapter contains all you need to know to grow 30 of my desert island edibles – vegetables, herbs, fruit and flowers – selected for their ease of growing and ability to adapt to small spaces. And because I enjoy eating as well as growing, I've included a handful of much-loved recipes too.

↑ A medley of squashes: winter squash 'Ute Indian', 'Delicata' and 'Sweet Dumpling', pumpkin 'Jack-Be-Little', and summer squash (dried) 'Tromboncino'.

Vegetable spotlights

When you grow your own, there are many seasonal 'firsts' to anticipate. Waxy early potatoes; baby carrots no bigger than your finger; the first explosive bite of a sun-warmed tomato. Simple pleasures, but some of the richest you will find, all bringing hope for the months ahead. Vegetables this fresh need little interference – in most cases just a drizzle of olive oil and a little seasoning. As well as new flavours, you'll discover a deep respect for your produce by knowing the journey these crops have been on to arrive at your plate.

Before you begin:

* Sowing/planting information is based on the various gardens I have known, where the last frost is generally mid-May and the first frost mid-October – USDA zone 8–9.
* Throughout this section you will see references to sowing **indoors**. This means inside with **heat** (unless otherwise stated). For example, an indoor windowsill, conservatory or heated greenhouse.
* Where appropriate, outdoor direct sowing times are listed – helpful for those without any indoor space. For **direct** sowing, see page 68.
* **Spacings** of seeds, modules and plants are given as a measurement (for example, 25 × 30cm/10 × 12in) where the first number is the spacing *within* a row and the second is the spacing *between* rows.

* '**Cover** seed' refers to whether to bury the seed in compost/soil or leave it on the surface uncovered. See page 62 for sowing depths.
* Minimum pot sizes are based on my experience growing in containers. Remember, bigger is generally better. See page 32 for more information on choosing your pot size.
* Look at How to plant a container, page 37, before planting or sowing pots.
* The majority of seed varieties suggested in this book are certified organic or produced by suppliers who grow to these standards. All are varieties that I know and trust. I've included a small number of non-organic varieties in my Top 30 where there is no organic alternative available but I feel the plant would be of particular benefit, for example if it has been specifically bred for a small space or has great flavour from previous taste trials.

Beetroot

I've led a lot of garden tours, and if ever I face a tough crowd, I bring out the beetroot. Slicing through raw roots of red, golden and stripy pink 'Chioggia' beets reveals their vibrant flesh; a striking contrast to the muddy exterior, sure to raise a collective gasp. Colourful beetroot lifts the spirits through the seasons, from the tender baby beets of early summer that slip from their skins after the briefest of boilings to their sweet, earthy counterparts, pulled tennis ball-size, for autumn roasting. Their pretty veined foliage is also edible, offering a nutritious leafy green similar to chard.

→ Colourful beetroot: 'Detroit Red', 'Chioggia' and 'Burpee's Golden'.

Growing tips

* An easy crop with few pest or disease issues.
* Multi-sow beetroot seed into modules (see below).
* For sowings in March, use the early variety 'Boltardy'.
* Keep well watered.

SOWING/PLANTING

Sow March to early July.

———

Sow indoors in modules with heat or no heat from mid-March (heat speeds things up). Cover the seed with compost.

———

Multi-sow modules – 3 seeds per module. Beetroot are 'cluster' seeds (1 seed is a cluster of seeds

→ Roasting beetroot whole with thyme.

bunched together), so more than 3 seedlings will germinate. Thin to 4 seedlings and plant out as a clump.

Alternatively, sow direct outdoors from April to early July (a final early July sowing will provide autumn crops). Make a drill (see page 68) or see Pots, page 111.

For continuous supplies, sow monthly from March to July.

Cover early sowings/plantings with fleece.

SPACINGS
(FOR POTS, SEE PAGE 114)

For good-sized beets, plant multi-sown modules 30cm (12in) between plants, 30cm (12in) between rows.

A closer spacing will yield smaller beets. I fit 5 multi-sown modules horizontally across my 1.2m (4ft) wide bed at a spacing of 25cm (10in) between plants, 30cm (12in) between rows.

For direct-sown crops, sow in drills, 5cm (2in) between plants, 30cm (12in) between rows.

HARVESTING

The longer beets are in the ground, the bigger they'll grow. Decide what size you like them, from the size of golf balls to tennis balls, and gently pull up the plant by its foliage. If sown in module clumps, twist individual beets from the clump in stages, leaving the others to grow on.

Roots keep well in the ground but remove before heavy frost.

VARIETIES

'Detroit Red', 'Burpee's Golden', 'Chioggia', 'Cheltenham Green Top', 'Egyptian Turnip Rooted', 'Bull's Blood'.

'Boltardy' is a bolt-resistant variety, good for early sowings, as cold weather can cause early flowering.

→ Freshly pulled beetroot 'Detroit Red', 'Chioggia' and 'Burpee's Golden'. Both the roots and leaves are edible.

↑ The young, edible leaves of beetroot 'Red Detroit'.

DESIGN TIPS

Grow 'Bull's Blood' for deep red, highly decorative leaves.

COMMON PROBLEMS

Generally problem-free.

Beet leaf miner (see Pests, page 80) may damage parts of leaves; simply cut out the damage if you are cooking with them.

Birds may peck small seedlings; cover with fleece or insect mesh if you anticipate a problem.

POTS

Pot size: Minimum depth 25cm (10in); minimum diameter 30cm (12in) for multiple beetroots.

Indoor windowsill: Yes – I grow single beetroots, not multi-sown clumps, in small terracotta pots (11cm/4in depth and diameter) on my windowsill. As they push out of the compost, both root and leaves make beautiful table decorations.

Fill containers with organic, peat-free multipurpose potting compost. Plant 5 or 6 modules to a 30cm (12in) diameter pot.

Alternatively, sow direct. Firm down the compost to create a flat surface using your hand or a piece of wood. Scatter seeds across (roughly 5cm/2in apart), covering lightly with a 2cm (¾in) layer of compost. Water well. Once germinated, thin to 5cm (2in) in all directions (thinned seedlings can be eaten as microgreens).

As plants grow, harvest some as babies while others grow bigger.

Consider earmarking several containers for successional sowing. Later sowings can be made in the same pot as early sowings once harvested – just replenish the top 1cm (¼in) with fresh compost.

Feed pots with organic liquid/homemade feed every 2 weeks (see page 36).

Carrots

Carrots should be grown to munch small, sweet and in situ – a mid-morning snack for the hungry gardener and any nearby children, who will revel in the theatre of pulling them up! The original carrot (from which today's orange carrot was bred) was purple and I grow a rainbow of varieties – orange, red, yellow, white, purple and some with purple skins and orange cores. Eat raw with dips as a cheerful summer crudité plate, and use the feathery foliage for carrot top pesto (try the recipe on page 176, substituting the rosemary for a bunch of fresh carrot tops and halving the amount of parsley).

→ Cover carrots with insect mesh to prevent carrot fly.

Growing tips

* Carrots require a little extra attention to succeed – they must be protected from carrot fly and slugs (see below).

* Carrots are best sown direct into beds and containers, as opposed to module-sown, as they don't respond well to root disturbance.

↑ Harvesting pot-grown 'Paris Market Atlas' carrots.

SOWING/PLANTING

Sow direct outside in drills or pots from March to mid July.

Early harvests in June are possible from end of March sowings (select from the early varieties listed below) but are less reliable than sowings from May onwards. Slugs are more rampant in early, damp months, so if you don't want to gamble, wait for drier weather in April or May.

SPACINGS
(FOR POTS, SEE PAGE 118)

Sow in drills 30cm (12in) apart. Sow 2–3 seeds per 1cm (¼in) and thin a month later to 1 seedling per 1cm (¼in) – see page 68.

HARVESTING

For baby carrots, harvest is possible from 8 weeks after sowing, from May–July. Much like beetroot, you decide on the size you like them. I leave July sowings to size up for nourishing autumnal stews.

VARIETIES

Earlies: 'Amsterdam Forcing' (can also be sown throughout the season).

Maincrop: 'Nantes 2/Milan' (can also be sown early), 'Rainbow Mix', 'Jaune Obtuse du Doubs', 'Cosmic Purple', 'Red Samurai' (F1).

Small: 'Paris Market Atlas' (good for smaller pots and windowsills).

→ Thin carrots on a still day, preferably in the evening, when there is no wind, so the scent does not carry and attract carrot fly.

DESIGN TIPS

Edge carrot containers with chives, which may deter carrot fly (although I still use insect mesh as well). Has the added bonus of looking pretty when chives flower.

If you have space, leave a few carrots in the ground/pot to overwinter – provided the roots don't rot, you will be rewarded with lacy, white umbels of flowers the following year (carrots are biennial, flowering and setting seed in their second year), which are particularly attractive to beneficial insects.

COMMON PROBLEMS

Carrot fly – use barrier protection (see Pests, page 80).

Slugs – tiny seedlings are vulnerable to slug damage, especially early in the year, which can easily wipe out a row over night. Aim to sow in drier weather or ensure the beds/pots are completely clear of weeds and foliage where slugs can hide.

Weeds – carrot seedlings are tiny and easily choked by weeds, even small ones. Use your fingers to pluck weeds out from between seedlings and hoe between rows.

POTS

Pot size: Minimum depth 20cm (8in); minimum diameter 20cm (8in).

Indoor windowsill: Yes – small round varieties work particularly well in smaller pots and will grow on sunny windowsills (see Varieties, page 117).

Carrots often grow better in pots than they do in the ground, as roots easily penetrate potting compost and you can shield them from pests. I use an old sink and a tin bath.

Sow direct into pots filled with organic, peat-free multipurpose potting compost. Firm down the compost to create a flat surface using your hand or a piece of wood. Sprinkle seed thinly on top and cover with a thin layer of compost. Water well and cover with insect mesh or fleece.

After 1 month, thin seedlings to 1cm (½in) apart. Once carrots are baby-sized, thin again, leaving the remainder to grow on for medium-sized roots.

Consider earmarking several containers for successional sowing. Later sowings can be made in the same pot as early sowings once harvested (just replenish the top 1cm (¼in) with fresh compost).

Feed pots with organic liquid/ homemade feed every 2 weeks (see page 36).

Chard

Arguably the most photogenic vegetable in the garden, with glossy green leaves and deep red, yellow, peach and hot pink stems and veins, resembling stained-glass windows when backlit with morning light. Even the ivory-stemmed Swiss chard looks glorious on a gloomy day. Earthy, slightly salty leaves are supplied for months on end and stand up well to milder winters. Simmer leaves and stems and serve with a drizzle of olive oil and a pinch of salt. This robust, spinach-like leaf tastes like it's doing you a whole lot of good!

Growing tips

* Also known as leaf beet, this is one of the easiest vegetables to grow.
* Tolerates some shade but is more abundant in full sun.
* Pick regularly to keep the supply coming. Leaves will grow huge if left unpicked and can become tough.
* In milder years, a July sowing will give good pickings through autumn. Plants then stop production through winter, putting on growth the following spring, when they can be picked until they send up a flowering stalk (great for cut flower arrangements!).
* Hard frost will kill plants.
* Can be grown as larger leaves to cook with or as baby leaves for salads.

SOWING/PLANTING

Sow late April to July.

Sow indoors in modules with heat or no heat from late April (heat speeds things up). Cover the seed with compost.

For cooking leaves, sow 2 seeds per module. As they are cluster seeds` (1 seed is a cluster of seeds bunched together), more than 2 seedlings will germinate. Thin to 2 seedlings per module and plant as a little clump. For baby leaves for salad, sow 4 seeds per module, thinning to 4 seedlings.

Alternatively, direct sow outdoors from April to early July (a final early July sowing will provide overwintering leaves).

If sowing direct, station sow
– make holes with your finger
at set intervals (see Spacings,
below) and drop in 4 seeds.
Cover the seed with compost.
Thin each clump to 2 seedlings
once they have their second set
of leaves. For smaller, baby leaves
for salad, thin to 4 seedlings.
See Spacings (below) and
Pots (page 122).

Cover early sowings/plantings
with fleece.

SPACINGS
(FOR POTS, SEE PAGE 122)

Plant modules 30cm (12in)
between plants, 30cm (12in)
between rows, 2 or 4 seedlings
per module, depending on leaf
size required.

For direct-sown crops in the
ground, sow seed according to
the spacings above.

→ The leaves of 'Flamingo' chard
with their bright pink stems.

→ 'Bright Yellow' chard, with its golden stems, is perfect as a baby leaf in salads.

HARVESTING

Holding the stem, peel the outer leaves gently from around the base of the plant as opposed to cutting them. Leave smaller leaves to grow on inside.

For baby leaves, use a sharp knife to gently cut off the outer leaves.

VARIETIES

'Rhubarb Chard', 'Five Colours', 'Rainbow', 'Flamingo', Swiss chard (white), 'Fordhook Giant', 'Bright Yellow', 'Peppermint'.

DESIGN TIPS

All types are beautiful in containers but the vivid pink 'Flamingo' chard is a real showstopper.

Don't feel you have to plant chard in neat rows – dot it through flower beds or use it to fill gaps in beds or pots.

COMMON PROBLEMS

Generally problem-free.

Beet leaf miner (see Pests, page 80), may damage parts of leaves; simply cut out the damage before cooking.

Birds may peck small seedlings; cover with fleece or insect mesh if you anticipate a problem.

POTS

Pot size: Minimum depth 20cm (8in); minimum diameter 28cm (11in) for larger plants.

Indoor windowsill: Yes – grow baby-leaf chard, see page 152.

See Design tips, above, and Window boxes, page 29, for planting combinations.

Fill containers with organic, peat-free multipurpose potting compost. For a full display, plant 3 modules (1 seedling per module) to a 30cm (12in) diameter pot. For smaller pots, plant 1 module per pot.

For baby leaves, sow direct into containers. Firm down the compost to create a flat surface, using your hand or a piece of wood. Scatter seeds across (roughly 8cm/3in apart), covering lightly with a 2cm (¾in) layer of compost. Water well. Once germinated, thin to 8cm (3in) in all directions (thinned seedlings can be eaten as microgreens).

Later sowings can be made in the same pot as early sowings (just replenish the top 1–2cm (¼–¾in) with fresh compost). Bring new plants on in modules to replace original plants as they tire.

Feed pots with organic liquid/homemade feed every 2 weeks (see page 36).

Courgettes & summer squash

Synonymous with summer, courgettes, with their yellow, trumpet-like blossoms, bring abundant harvests. Flowers stuffed with ricotta and encased in light, crispy batter are one of the vegetable garden's most precious gifts. Although less glamorous, the fruits themselves have an understated beauty, their soft, downy skins streaked with varying shades of green or golden-yellow. Long, round, swan-necked or scalloped-edged, they offer a beautiful assortment of shapes and colours, all markedly improved with olive oil, sea salt and a squeeze of lemon.

Growing tips

* Courgettes need plenty of sunshine.
* They are thirsty plants, so keep well watered and mulch/top-dress pots (see below).
* Courgettes are also hungry. Add compost or well-rotted manure to beds in the winter before planting. And an extra helping in planting holes won't go amiss.
* One plant goes a long way. For a family of three (plus friends), I grow one golden variety, one 'Romanesco' or striped green type, and a 'Tromboncino' or other pretty-shaped summer squash for pure indulgence.
* Frost kills the plants.

← Freshly picked courgettes 'Gold Rush' and 'Striato di Napoli' with 'Tromboncino' squash.

↓ Courgette 'Striato di Napoli', with a female flower attached and the fruit beginning to form.

IN DEPTH: COURGETTE FLOWERS

Courgette plants produce both male and female flowers, and both are edible. Male flowers form on long, thin stems, while females have a swelling at the base where the fruit is forming. Pollen is transferred, usually by bees or other pollinating insects, from the male flower to the female, and fruit starts to form. Male flowers dominate early in the season – pick them to eat. Once your plant is producing male and female flowers, both can be cropped (the latter with a baby courgette attached) but don't pick them all to eat or you'll have no courgettes. Leave a few males behind to pollinate the forming females.

SOWING/PLANTING

Sow mid-April to early June.

———

Sow indoors in 9cm (3½in) pots (or similar) in mid- to late April. They like warmer temperatures for germination, ideally 21–35°C (70–95°F).

———

Make a hole 1–2cm (¼–¾in) deep, drop in the seed and cover the seed with compost. Sow 2 seeds per pot to ensure germination and thin to the strongest seedling once established.

———

Alternatively, sow direct outdoors from mid-late May to early June. Sow 2–3 seeds per station (3cm/1in deep) and thin to the strongest seedling once established.

———

Don't be tempted to sow too early (earlier than mid-April indoors or mid-May outside), as you'll be battling the cold. Similarly, don't plant out until the last frost has passed, from mid- to late May.

———

If your plant outgrows its pot, don't be tempted to place it outside too early. Pot it on to a larger pot before planting out in its final destination.

———

Harden off plants (see page 66) and cover with fleece after planting if you want them to establish more quickly.

———

← Harvest courgettes by slicing the stem off at the base with a sharp knife.

SPACINGS
(FOR POTS, SEE OPPOSITE)

Leave 90cm (3ft) between plants, 90cm (3ft) between rows.

HARVESTING

Use a sharp knife, slicing the courgette stem off at the base, as opposed to twisting or pulling.

Keep picking the fruits or production will slow.

Take extra care when harvesting flowers – they can easily tear.

Pick fruits when they are small and tender. You'll likely end up with some guilt-inducing whoppers. Don't be afraid to compost these; they will be returned to your soil.

VARIETIES

'Cocozelle', 'Romanesco', 'Gold Rush', 'Striato di Napoli', 'Floridor' F1, 'Sunburst' F1, 'Tromboncino', 'Piccolo' F1 (good for pots).

IN DEPTH: TROMBONCINO

Fruits grow into trombone-shaped (and -sized) squashes in autumn, and look spectacular dangling from supports. Sadly, they have no flavour at this size. Harvest small (10–13cm/4–5in) for sweet, nutty squashes through the summer months. They are perfect for training upwards in a small space – gently guide the growth tip towards the support, tying the stem on loosely with twine in a figure-of-eight knot. The plant sends out tendrils to grip on with. Keep tying in the stems to the support as the plant climbs. If using a tepee, wrap string/twine around the canes in a spiral, twisting around each cane as you go. This will give you something to tie the plant to, as opposed to just the canes.

DESIGN TIPS

Interplant courgettes and summer squash with nasturtiums. Nasturtiums hold their own against courgettes and squash, which like to spread out, and attract pollinators for fruit setting.

COMMON PROBLEMS

No fruit or small rotting fruit can be caused by poor pollination. If cool summers lead to a lack of pollinators, it's possible to hand-pollinate plants yourself (although I've never had to do this – plants normally sort themselves out). Remove a male flower, peel back the petals and press the anther containing pollen into the centre of the female flowers. You can use 1 male flower to pollinate several females.

A lack of female flowers, and therefore fruit, may be because the plant is stressed. Keep well fed and watered and follow the correct timings above.

Powdery mildew later in the season (see Diseases, page 83).

Pollen beetle. These little black insects feed on flower pollen and are only an issue if you want to eat the flowers. Once you've picked the flowers, give them a gentle shake or leave them outside in a shaded spot to let the insects escape.

POTS

Pot size: Minimum depth 25cm (10in); minimum diameter 45cm (18in) – deeper (45cm/18in) and wider (50–60cm/20–24in) would be better.

Indoor windowsill: No.

Choose a large container (a 60cm (24in) diameter pot is best). Courgettes like to spread their roots, and small pots dry out fast. Grow one plant per pot in organic, peat-free, multipurpose potting compost. Top-dress with garden/worm compost or well-rotted manure for extra nutrients and to conserve moisture.

They will also grow in organic, peat-free grow bags. Buy two bags and stack one on top of the other for better yield (see page 33). Plant 2 plants per set of grow bags.

Stand in a sunny spot, keep well watered and feed pots with organic liquid/homemade feed every 2 weeks (see page 36).

Kale

Kale is divisive: tough and bitter to some, deeply nourishing to others. To fall in love with kale, you need to grow the right varieties. Cover all the bases with three types, each offering their own rugged beauty and flavours. 'Red Russian' kale: soft, sweet and mild; cavolo nero: blistered, rich and earthy; curly kale: frilly, peppery and bitter. Kale is one of the easier brassicas to grow, offering up nutritious greens in early spring when not much else is about. And the flavours improve the colder it gets. Blanch, then swish with garlic and olive oil or bake kale chips (crisps) in the oven to bring out the sweetness – you'll always wish you'd made more.

→ A bunch of different kales: 'Red Russian', 'Nero di Toscana', 'Dwarf Green Curled' and 'True Siberian'.

Growing tips

* Kale grows almost all year round. Traditionally, it plugged the 'hungry gap', where winter produce finished and spring crops had yet to begin (a time when starvation was a genuine concern).
* Works well as a second planting, following spring and early summer crops.
* Tolerates a little (not full) shade and is frost-hardy.
* Protect against cabbage white butterfly and birds (see below).
* Avoid growing kale in the same spot year on year, as diseases can build up.

SOWING/PLANTING

Sow April to early July.

Sow indoors in modules from April. Cover the seed with compost. I favour a June/July sowing – plants will crop well in late summer and autumn, giving occasional winter harvests, before picking up growth the following spring. They flower in March/April. The flowers and shoots are delicious.

Sow 2 seeds per module, thinning to 1 seedling.

Direct outdoor sowings easily succumb to pests, so even if you have no indoor space, start in modules outside from June, covering trays with insect mesh.

Plant out after a month when the roots have fully filled out the module. Sink up to the first leaves to add stability.

SPACINGS
(FOR POTS, SEE PAGE 130)

Leave 45cm (18in) between plants, 45cm (18in) between rows.

HARVESTING

Pick the leaves regularly to keep plants productive. As with chard, don't cut the leaves off. Instead, peel the lower, outer leaves from around the base of the plant.

Remove any yellow, damaged leaves, for composting.

VARIETIES

'Nero di Toscana', 'Red Russian', 'Dazzling Blue', 'Dwarf Green Curled', 'Red Curled', 'Westland Winter', 'True Siberian'.

Perennial kales, such as the varieties 'Daubenton' and 'Taunton Deane', are fantastic options for those with more space – they can grow to 2m (6½ft) tall and wide, so are best in open ground unless you have a huge pot! There's no need for resowing, as they produce an endless supply of delicious leaves for five or six years and are easy to propagate from stem cuttings.

DESIGN TIPS

The deep purple-black foliage of cavolo nero contrasts beautifully with the burnt orange of nasturtiums, calendula and French marigolds. Fill the gaps between plants with these edible flowers.

The dusty pink and turquoise leaves of 'Red Russian' kale are lovely alongside white-flowering garlic chives.

COMMON PROBLEMS

Kale is reliable and problem-free compared with other brassicas.

Cabbage white butterflies and birds can be an issue (see Pests, page 80, and Protecting your crops, page 71).

Cabbage whitefly – these small winged insects collect on the underside of leaves, taking flight in big clouds when the leaf is touched. Young whitefly resembling scales remain on the leaf and can be washed off before eating. Plants can cope with large infestations. Insect mesh will prevent them.

POTS

Pot size: Minimum depth 20cm (8in); minimum diameter 28cm (11in).

Indoor windowsill: Yes – baby leaves (see page 152) or microgreens for salad (see page 26).

Top tips

'Ornamental' kale is one for the foodies among you. Smaller and more like a cabbage in form, ornamental kales were traditionally added to borders for their winter colour. But the inner leaves are beautifully sweet and tender. Experiment with a range of varieties in hot pinks and creamy whites. Try 'Red Peacock' F1 and 'White Peacock' F1 with their pretty feathered edges. Their compact size makes them perfect for pots.

→ Kale 'Red Russian' looks pretty growing in a pot.

These bold, textured plants make wonderful backdrops to containers (see pages 38–9 for design ideas).

Aim for 1 plant per pot (30cm/12in diameter) for good-sized leaves. Wider containers can be planted with several compact varieties (a combination of 'Dwarf Green Curled', 'Red Russian' and a compact nasturtium works well) but the less space there is, the smaller the leaves will be.

Fill containers with organic, peat-free multipurpose compost. I find potting modules into 9cm (3½in) pots to size up, before planting in their final larger pot, works best. Water well and feed pots with organic liquid/homemade feed every 2 weeks (see page 36).

To ward off pigeons and cabbage white butterflies, make a frame within the pot with canes, topped with 9cm (3½in) pots, and drape over butterfly netting or insect mesh.

Smaller varieties (dwarf kale and 'Red Russian') grow to around 50–60cm (20–24in) tall; larger varieties ('Nero di Toscana' and 'Red Curled') to around 90cm (3ft).

If you only have one or two plants, it is possible to avoid having netting and pick off caterpillars by hand, but you will need to check for them daily.

Potatoes

Freshly dug early potatoes with a generous knob of butter and fresh spring herbs, like chives, mint and parsley, are comfort food at its best. Rummaging around to discover a fully formed potato buried in the earth fills any adult with a childlike wonder that never diminishes. And the good news is, this is simple to achieve, even in an old compost sack.

→ Elegant potato flowers.

↓ Planter bags are ideal for growing potatoes in a confined space.

Growing tips

* Potatoes fall into two major groups – earlies and maincrop. Earlies are divided again into first earlies, cropping in June/July, and second earlies, cropping in July/August. Maincrops are ready from August to October. Earlies are what we refer to as 'new potatoes'. Maincrops can be eaten fresh or stored.
* In small spaces, opt for earlies – they are planted closer together, taking up less room. Alternatively, use bags or containers, particularly if you want maincrops, so that they don't take up valuable space in your beds.
* If tubers near the surface are exposed to light, they turn green and are poisonous. Earthing up prevents this (see page 134).
* Potatoes need a sunny spot and consistent watering. Keep the soil damp but do not drench.

SOWING/PLANTING

Grow from seed potatoes, which look like potatoes you buy to eat, except they are certified disease- and virus-free, which is important.

For extra early crops, you can chit seed potatoes as soon as you receive them in late winter (January/February). See Give a chit?, page 136.

As a general rule, plant first earlies mid- to late March, second earlies early to mid-April, and maincrop mid- to late April. In colder areas, you may need to wait longer to plant.

Planting in containers/bags means you don't have to let the ground warm up and you can start earlier, but I'd still recommend you get going in March. See Potatoes in bags, page 136–7.

Traditionally, a trench was dug for potatoes, but for less soil disturbance, plant in individual holes made with a hand trowel, 10–15cm (4–6in) deep. Plant tubers with shoots facing up. Aim for 3–4 shoots per chitted tuber; the others can be rubbed off with your fingers. Be careful not to knock off the remaining shoots when planting.

Cover plantings with horticultural fleece.

SPACINGS
(FOR POTS, SEE OPPOSITE)

First earlies: 30cm (12in) between plants, 30cm (12in) between rows.

Second earlies: 30cm (12in) between plants, 45cm (18in) between rows.

Maincrops: 38cm (15in) between plants, 75cm (30in) between rows.

EARTHING UP

Drawing soil up around the base of plants as they grow prevents tubers going green.

When plants are 15cm (6in) tall, use a hoe or rake to draw soil from either side of the row, around the stems of the potatoes, creating a ridge. Cover the lower leaves, leaving just the tops uncovered.

Repeat the process as plants grow – your final ridge will be around 20cm (8in) tall.

For minimal soil disturbance in no-dig beds, you could achieve the same effect by piling additional compost around plants.

The same principle is replicated in pots and bags by the addition of more compost.

← Harvesting early potatoes that have been grown in a bag.

COMMON PROBLEMS

Late blight affects maincrop varieties (see Diseases, page 83).

A late spring frost can knock back the foliage but the tubers should be protected underground and will send up new growth. Use fleece for protection.

HARVESTING

Earlies are ready when the plants are in flower. They are best eaten fresh, still tasting of the soil! Not suitable for storing.

Maincrops are ready when the leaves start to yellow and die back. If storing maincrops, cut back the foliage and leave the potatoes in the ground for a week for the skins to harden.

In raised beds, it's possible to use a trowel to ease out plants, as the compost is soft. In open ground, use a digging fork, taking care not to pierce the tubers.

For harvesting in bags/pots, see pages 136–7.

VARIETIES

Trialling vegetable varieties was a big part of my work with Raymond Blanc. The potato taste test was mammoth – Raymond was on a quest to find the perfect potato, best suited to purée, mash, roasting, chipping, steaming and boiling. No one should have to eat that many carbs in one sitting, but it has guided my selection ever since.

Organic: 'Maris Bard' (first early), 'Colleen' (first early), 'Charlotte' (second early), 'Nicola' (second early), 'Golden Wonder' (maincrop), 'Sarpo Mira' (maincrop) – blight-resistant.

Non-organic: 'Swift' (first early and one of the fastest-maturing types), 'Red Duke of York' (first early), 'International Kidney' (second early/early maincrop), 'BF15' (second early), 'Belle de Fontenay' (second early), 'Ratte' (early maincrop), 'Pink Fir Apple' (late maincrop).

DESIGN TIPS

Potato flowers are unexpectedly elegant; little soft pink and violet stars, or creamy white with saffron-yellow stamens.

POTS

Pot size: Minimum depth 30cm (12in); minimum diameter 30cm (12in) for larger plants. Bigger is definitely better – aim for the capacity of a 40-litre (10 ½ gallon) compost sack – 3 tubers to a sack works well.

Potatoes in bags

If you're short on space, potatoes grow happily in bags or makeshift containers. I've even grown them successfully in an old dustbin. You can buy special potato planter bags, but a reused empty compost sack works just as well. As a general rule, each tuber needs 8 litres (2 gallons) of potting compost. I've found three tubers in a 40-litre (10½-gallon) sack works well. They are wonderfully easy to grow this way.

Planting step-by-step

What you'll need:

Seed potatoes (3 per bag)

Egg box or seed tray

Multipurpose organic, peat-free potting compost

40-litre (10½-gallon) bag/planter

GIVE A CHIT?

Chitting – placing seed potatoes in a cool, bright, frost-free place to encourage shooting before planting – is thought to increase yields and produce an earlier crop, particularly with first and second early potatoes. But the jury's out as to whether this is necessary. For me, it comes down to space. If suitable chitting spaces like windowsills, porches, conservatories or greenhouses are full of other seedlings early in the year, don't bother. Commercial growers don't chit, and I've grown spuds perfectly well without too. If you do have the room, then it is worth trying for the promise of bigger yields.

1 Start the chitting process six weeks before planting (see pages 132–5 for timings and varieties). Place potatoes in an egg box or seed tray in a cool, bright place, around 10°C (50°F). A lack of light and too much warmth produces leggy shoots. Put the end with the most eyes (little buds that turn into shoots) facing up. When ready to plant, leave 3–4 shoots on the tubers, rubbing off the rest with your fingers, otherwise you'll end up with lots of small potatoes.

2 Plant your potatoes from March. Place 20cm (8in) of compost in the bottom of a 40-litre (10½ gallon) bag (be sure to poke drainage holes in the bottom of the bag, if not already present, using scissors or a knife). Roll down the sides of the bag to less than ⅓ of its height to allow light in. Plant 3 tubers (shoots facing up) into the compost, a hand's width apart. Add another 10–20cm (4–8in) of compost to cover the tubers. Water the compost, so that it is damp, not wet.

3 When the shoots are 10–15cm (4–6in) tall, add more compost, drawing it around the stems and leaving only the tops of the foliage exposed. Roll up the sides of the bag when you add more compost. Repeat this as the plants grow until you reach 5cm (2in) from the top of the bag. Then allow the plants to grow freely.

4 Place the bag somewhere sunny and sheltered. Ensure there is good airflow around the bag, to prevent fungal diseases. Keep well-watered – consistent watering is needed for good yields, as well as feeding every two weeks with organic liquid/homemade feed (see page 36). If frost is due, cover the bag with horticultural fleece or move to a frost-free spot.

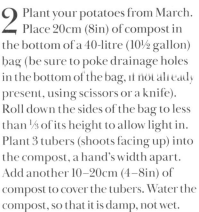

5 Early potatoes are ready to harvest when the plants are in flower, and maincrops once the foliage starts to fade. Feel around in the bag for tubers to check if they are a good size for you to harvest. Alternatively, take the plunge and empty the whole bag into a bucket/ trug, as in this photograph. The used compost can be added to pots, garden beds or compost.

Radish

One of the earliest glimmers of colour in spring soil, the crisp crunch of a rosy radish is a cheerful way to wave goodbye to winter. Serve whole with green tops attached, alongside bowls of butter and salt for dipping. They offer some of the quickest returns in the vegetable garden, ready in four weeks when temperatures warm. Their size makes them perfect for small gardens, pots and windowsills. Big and bold in comparison are winter radishes: large, fiery roots that are slower growing and ready in autumn – perfect for pickling and Asian dishes.

Growing tips

* Keep the soil/compost moist to prevent bolting and split, spongy roots. Do not allow to dry out.
* Protect against flea beetle (see Pests, page 80).

SOWING/PLANTING

Spring/summer radish
Sow February to August.

For the earliest crops (in April), sow indoors in modules in mid-February, to plant out in March.

Multi-sow seeds – sow 5 seeds per module, cover the seed with compost and thin to 4 seedlings once germinated. Plant out as a clump, covering with fleece.

For continuous supplies, sow monthly from February to August, but sowings after April battle with flea beetle – transition from fleece to insect mesh as protection from May.

Alternatively, direct sow outdoors from March to August. Make a drill (see page 68) and see Spacings (below).

Use fleece or insect mesh throughout the season to stop flea beetle damaging leaves.

Winter radish
Direct sow outdoors from late July to mid-August. Any sowings before July will bolt. Make a drill (see page 68).

Cover with insect mesh to stop flea beetle.

SPACINGS
(FOR POTS, SEE PAGE 140)

Spring/summer radish
Plant multi-sown modules at 15cm (6in) between plants, 15cm (6in) between rows.

For direct-sown crops, thin to 1 seedling per 3cm (1in).

Winter radish
10cm (4in) between plants, 30cm (12in) between rows.

→ Harvesting the spring/summer radish 'Cherry Belle'.

HARVESTING

Pick spring/summer radish when young (4 weeks on average) and the shoulders are nudging out of the soil.

Pick winter radish in autumn. Round varieties can reach tennis-ball size. The roots of daikon/mooli types can reach 25cm (10in) in length, so aim long! They will hold in the ground until the hard frosts arrive.

Top tips

RADISH PODS

The seed pods of radishes are a spicy treat and great in stir-fries, salads and quick pickles. Grow 'Rat-tail' and 'Munchen Bier' varieties specifically for their pods, not roots.

VARIETIES

Spring/summer radish: 'French Breakfast', 'Cherry Belle', 'Rudi'.

———

Winter radish: 'Round Black Spanish', 'Rosa', 'Minowase'*, 'Red Flesh Mild Tricolour' (not strictly a winter radish but I find it grows well from a late July/early August sowing).

———

*'Minowase' is a mooli or daikon radish (Japanese radishes with long pointed roots), which are great for pickling. Seed packets tell you to sow from April, but I find sticking to winter radish sowing times works best.

———

DESIGN TIPS

The rosy shoulders of radishes look pretty growing on an indoor windowsill, where flea beetle is less of a threat.

———

COMMON PROBLEMS

Flea beetle (see Pests, page 80).

———

POTS

Spring/summer radish:
Pot size: Minimum depth 15cm (6in); minimum diameter 20cm (8in).

———

Indoor windowsill: Yes.

———

Winter radish:
Pot size: Minimum depth 30cm (12in); minimum diameter 30cm (12in).

———

Indoor windowsill: No.

———

Radish are the perfect pot crop. Choose rounded varieties like 'Cherry Belle' and 'Rudi', as opposed to the longer 'French Breakfast'. Their shallow roots mean you can grow them in containers that will easily fit on a windowsill (indoor or out). Summer radish will tolerate a little shade and can be grown on the dappled edges of pots housing taller crops like kale – but you'll still need to protect them from flea beetle.

———

For steady spring/summer supplies, earmark 3 pots for radishes. Fill the first pot with organic, peat-free multipurpose compost. Firm down the compost to create a flat surface using your hand or a piece of wood. Sprinkle seed evenly over the surface, roughly 3cm (1in) apart, covering lightly with a 1–2cm (¼–¾in) layer of compost. Water well and keep the compost moist, checking daily. If the pot is outside, cover with a piece of fleece or insect mesh. Once germinated, thin the seedlings to 3cm (1in). Feed pots with organic liquid/homemade feed every 2 weeks (see page 36).

———

Repeat this in the second and third pots, sowing one pot every 10–14 days. Once the first pot is harvested, add a 1cm (¼in) sprinkling of fresh compost and resow straight into it, doing the same with the other pots once cropped.

———

Winter radish needs more space. You will only be able to fit 4–5 roots into a 30cm (12in) pot.

———

Recipe
Quick pickled radish

Ingredients

1 bunch of radishes

2 tablespoons apple cider vinegar

2 tablespoons honey or sugar

pinch of salt

To increase the recipe, just use equal amounts of vinegar to honey/sugar. You can add any preferred herbs and spices to this basic pickle liquid – I like chopped tarragon, mint or a sprinkle of chive flowers to garnish. Also works well with thinly sliced carrots, courgettes and beetroot.

→ The quick-pickling and colourful radish 'Red Flesh Mild Tricolour'.

Adds a delicious crunch to salads, sandwiches, soups and Asian dishes.

1 Discard the leaves and roots, and finely slice the radishes.

2 Mix the vinegar with the honey/sugar in a bowl until the honey/sugar dissolves.

3 Add the sliced radishes with a pinch of salt, and leave to marinate for 10 minutes.

4 Eat immediately.

French & runner beans

The decorative seeds of French and runner beans look too precious to bury beneath the earth. Runner beans were originally brought to the UK as an ornamental plant due to their glorious flowers. I grow them over a metal archway to create a colourful entrance to my plot, plus training them up a support saves on space. French and runner beans can provide two delicious crops: fresh pods in summer and dried beans for winter use.

Growing tips

* French and runner beans are killed by frost.
* They need plenty of water, especially in dry summers, and consistent watering is needed once the flowers open, in order for beans to form.

← An arch planted with runner bean 'Scarlet Emperor'.

* They're hungry plants – add garden compost or well-rotted manure to beds in the winter before planting. And an extra helping in planting holes won't go amiss.
* Beans should cling to their sticks/canes without assistance, but if not, loosely tie stems on with twine in a figure-of-eight knot to get them started.
* Pinch out the tops when plants reach the top of their sticks/canes so that the plants bush out.
* The flowers are edible.

SOWING/PLANTING

Sow in May/June.

Sow indoors in 9cm (3½in) pots or equivalent from mid- to late May to mid-June. The inner tubes of toilet rolls work well but plants quickly outgrow these, so you'll need to plant out sooner than you would in pots. Plant with the cardboard.

Make a hole with your finger 5cm (2in) deep, to your second knuckle, and cover the seed with compost. These plants like warmer temperatures for germination, ideally 16–30°C (61–86°F).

Sow 2 seeds per pot for runners, and thin to 1 as soon as they're up and away. Sow 3 per pot for French beans and thin to 2 per pot. Climbing French beans aren't as dense as runners, which is why you can plant 2 per stick/cane.

Plant out after 3 weeks or after the last frost, making a hole with a hand trowel.

Alternatively, direct sow outdoors in late May to June. Construct a tepee or supports beforehand, and sow more seed than you need, as seedlings are vulnerable to slugs. Sow 3 or 4 seeds per stick, thinning (as above) only once plants are more robust.

← The speckled pink pods of the climbing French bean 'Stokkievitsboon'.

SPACINGS
(FOR POTS, SEE OPPOSITE)

For spacing beans on tepees, see Making a tepee, pages 74–5. The principle is the same in the ground as it is in pots: aim for a 45–60cm (18–24in) diameter tepee, depending on bed size.

If growing up a trellis or netting fixed to a wall or fence, space plants 20cm (8in) apart.

My metal garden arch is 40cm (16in) wide on each side. I plant 3 runner bean plants either side for abundant flowers and foliage.

HARVESTING

Runner beans
Aim to pick pods when they're 15cm (6in) long. If beans inside their pods are starting to swell, they're past their best for eating. Beans are easily missed in among the foliage, so look closely. The more you pick, the more productive the plants will be.

French beans
Pick fresh when 10cm (4in) long, or if growing as a dried bean for winter, leave unpicked for harvest in autumn. Borlotto and Soissons varieties are best shelled and eaten fresh or used as dried beans, as opposed to eating the whole pod.

Drying pods
Both French and runner beans can be eaten dried (the latter like butter beans). Pick earlier pods fresh, leaving beans formed later on the plant for drying.

Simply leave pods on the plant until they dry out (usually in October). You want the pods to feel dry and crispy as you pull them apart. Harvest on a dry day. If wet weather is due, harvest and bring indoors to dry further – spread out on trays with good airflow.

Store in a cool dry place in airtight containers. Some beans can be eaten and others saved for seed for next year (see Seed saving, pages 76–7).

VARIETIES

Runner beans: 'Scarlet Emperor', 'Lady Di' (stringless), 'Prizewinner', 'Czar', 'Hestia' (dwarf, pretty in pots).

French beans: 'Cobra', 'Blauhilde' (purple), 'Neckargold' (yellow), 'Cherokee Trail of Tears', 'Helios' (dwarf), 'Purple Teepee' (dwarf).

→ 'Stokkievitsboon' is a Borlotto-type bean which is delicious in soups and stews. To avoid toxins, soak the beans overnight, boil for 10 minutes, then simmer until cooked.

For great-flavoured dried beans: 'Borlotto di Fuoco', 'Borlotto Lingua di Fuoco Dwarf', 'Soissons Gros Blanc à Rames', 'Stokkievitsboon'.

Note: purple-podded beans turn green on cooking.

DESIGN TIPS

For the prettiest French bean flowers, opt for 'Blauhilde' or 'Cherokee Trail of Tears'.

In their natural habitat, these beans scramble up trees in mountainous forests. If you have an established fruit tree in a pot (with an open structure), try training a runner bean plant up it.

Use natural materials for structures, like willow and hazel (see Grow up, pages 72–3).

Beans look beautiful climbing walls and fences. Hang jute bean netting 10cm (4in) from the wall to allow them to climb more freely.

COMMON PROBLEMS

Slugs are the main enemy of direct-sown beans (see Pests, page 80). To offer plants the best chance, sow indoors and plant out when larger.

POTS

Pot size: Minimum depth 30cm (12in) – deeper is better; minimum diameter 50cm (20in).

Indoor windowsill: No.

Both runner and French beans grow well in pots filled with organic, peat-free, multipurpose potting compost, provided the containers are large and receive plenty of water – always keep them moist. Feed pots with organic liquid/homemade feed every 2 weeks (see page 36). For how to make a tepee in a pot, see pages 74–5.

Dwarf runner and French beans are well suited to pots and window boxes without the need for supports (see Varieties, above). Space 35cm (14in) apart in all directions.

Salad leaves

A garden salad is a work of art, only achieved by growing your own. Lettuces provide great crunch and are some of the prettiest crops you can grow, but don't stop there. Add punchy flavoured leaves like sorrel and rocket, soft herbs, edible flowers and microgreens to complete your masterpiece. Happily, there is salad for every season.

Growing tips (lettuce)

* I use Charles Dowding's method for growing lettuce and winter leaves. No one knows more about salad growing than Charles! He has dedicated various books and courses to the subject (see Resources, pages 220–1). His spacings and techniques have served me well for many years. Rather than harvesting whole lettuce heads, leaves are picked from around the outside of the plant, eliminating the need to keep resowing. Charles's method of three to four sowings throughout the season gives constant supplies.
* Certain varieties are better suited to this method (see Varieties, opposite).
* Lettuce needs to be kept moist in dry weather. Water in the mornings to avoid a slug midnight feast.
* For other salad leaves, see page 148.

SOWING/PLANTING (LETTUCE)

Sow indoors in modules from mid-February to March, and early June to mid-July for supplies into autumn. For winter supplies undercover, sow early September.

Sow 2 seeds per module, thinning to 1 once germinated. Lettuce seed is tiny, so make only a shallow dent with your finger, no deeper than 2cm (¾in). Lightly cover the seed with a little compost.

Plant out the seedlings after (roughly) a month.

Cover early plantings with horticultural fleece.

I sow 20 lettuces per two adults – this keeps us going for several months until the next sowing is ready to be harvested.

SPACINGS
(FOR POTS, SEE PAGE 152)

Plant modules 22cm (8½in) between plants, 22cm (8½in) between rows.

↑ Harvest individual leaves from the base of a lettuce for a continuous supply.

HARVESTING

Start with the bottom leaves and work up, gently peeling away from the main stem with your fingers.

Discard any damaged leaves – this will happen less once plants get going.

Pick hard each time, leaving a clump of 6–8 leaves in the centre of the plant.

Over time the stems will thicken up and elongate, and the plants will look like little trees.

VARIETIES

Choose loose-leaf, Cos and batavian types for Charles's growing methods. My favourites include: 'Cerbiatta', 'Navarra', 'Grenoble Red', 'Flashy Butter Oak', 'Really Red Deer Tongue', 'Red Solix', 'Till', 'Emerald Oak', 'Little Leprechaun', 'Paris Island Cos'.

Lettuces harvested as whole heads are sometimes a treat (leave 25cm (10in) between plants, 30cm (12in) between rows):

Butterheads: 'Optima', 'Suzan', 'Marvel of Four Seasons'.
Crisphead: 'Reine de Glaces'.
Cos: 'Little Gem' – delicious sliced in half and griddled on the barbecue (space 20cm (8in) between plants, 20cm (8in) between rows).

More salad leaves: Summer

SUMMER PURSLANE

Succulent, juicy texture. Refreshing. Loves the heat. Sow indoors in modules from May to early July, or make a 1cm (¼in) deep drill and sow direct into the ground, with rows 22cm (8½in) apart. Space modules (or thin seedlings to) 10cm (4in) apart. Once 10cm (4in) tall, pick small shoots with a cluster of leaves at the ends of the stems to encourage regrowth. Can be grown densely as baby leaves on a windowsill (see Pots, page 152).

NEW ZEALAND SPINACH

Regular spinach quickly bolts in the heat of the summer and is best grown in spring or autumn/winter. New Zealand spinach loves heat and will provide fleshy cut-and-come-again leaves for salad or cooking.

Two plants per person is enough. A great ground-cover plant, slot into gaps of bare soil. Sow indoors in modules or small pots in April, and plant out after danger of frost has passed in late May. Alternatively, sow direct in May, spacing 30cm (12in) between plants × 60cm (24in) between rows.

FRENCH SORREL

Lemon sherbet-flavoured leaf. Although it's a perennial, I sow French sorrel every year, as it tends to run to seed in the second spring. Sow indoors in modules from March to June, 3 seeds per module. Plant as a clump. Space 30cm (12in) apart; 2 or 3 plants will be enough. Not a fan of hot, dry conditions. Keep well watered. Will tolerate light shade and can be picked into the colder months. Also look out for buckler-leaved sorrel, with smaller leaves even more suited to salads and a favourite among chefs.

Cool season salad leaves: Spring/ Autumn/Winter

If sown in late summer, these leaves can provide pickings through autumn/winter and a bounty when they pick up growth in spring. Some can be sown as early as February for early spring crops. Cover early sowings with fleece.

SPINACH

Use young and raw in salads, or leave to grow larger to cook. Sow from February (indoors) or March to April (outside) and again in late July to mid-August for overwintering plants that come to life the following spring. Select early varieties ('Early Prickly Seed') for February sowings and winter varieties ('Giant Winter') for overwintering. Sow 3 seeds per module, spacing 25 × 25cm

↓ The succulent leaves of fast-growing summer purslane make a nutritious addition to a salad.

(10 × 10in). Pot plantings can be closer. Suitable as baby leaves on a windowsill (see Pots, page 152).

LAND CRESS

Punchy, watercress-like flavour and pretty serrated leaves. Sow indoors in modules in early August for overwintering. Thin to 1 seeding per module. Space plants 22 × 22cm (8½in × 8½in). Pick the outer leaves first.

CLAYTONIA (WINTER PURSLANE)

Mild, juicy leaf. Also known as miner's lettuce (allegedly, miners ate this plant to ward off scurvy caused by a vitamin C deficiency). Forms succulent lily pad-like leaves with elegant white flowers – all edible – in late spring. Sowing, planting and harvesting as for land cress (see above).

↓ Pea shoots grown on a windowsill make a delicious microgreen.

CORN SALAD

Mild, nutty little rosettes. Also known as lamb's lettuce or mâche. Sow at the end of August, 1 seed per module, and plant out 15cm (6in) between plants, or direct sow 5–10cm (2–4in) between plants, 30cm (12in) between rows. Crop the central, upper rosette (not too low), allowing new ones to form below. Mildew can spoil this crop if it dries out so keep the soil moist. Varieties: 'Vit' and 'D'Orlanda'.

ASIAN GREENS

Fast-growing, spicy leaves, including colourful mustards and mizuna. Eat the leaves small in salads or grow bigger to cook. Mustards are very hardy. Varieties: 'Green in Snow', 'Giant Red', 'Purple Frills' and mixes of Asian leaves. Sow indoors in modules in August, 3 seeds per module for salad, thin to 1 seeding for cooking leaves. Space 22cm (8½in) between plants, 22cm (8½in) between rows. Protect from flea beetle (see page 82). Suitable as a baby-leaf crop on a windowsill (see Pots, page 152), and red mustard makes a delicious microgreen (see page 28).

PEA SHOOTS

Peas are multi-sown (3–5 to a module) indoors from mid-February to March. Plant out at 25cm (10in) between plants, 25cm (10in) between rows. When plants reach around 30cm (12in), pinch out the top shoots (5–10cm/2–4in) to harvest. Sweet and crunchy, they taste almost as good as fresh peas! This encourages sideshoots, which are cropped at 5cm (2in) in subsequent harvests until late May/early June. Also suitable on windowsills as a microgreen (see page 28). For microgreen pea shoots, use 'dwarf' pea varieties. For module-sown shoots, both tall and dwarf pea varieties are suitable.

ROCKET

There are two types: wild rocket, with thin, serrated leaves, yellow flowers and spicy flavour, and salad rocket, with larger leaves, white flowers and a milder flavour. Pick both young – the bigger the leaves, the hotter they become. Both grow best in cool conditions. Sow in early August for overwintered/spring crops. Either sow direct in pots as a cut-and-come-again crop for smaller leaves or space module-grown

→ The spicy leaves of mixed Asian greens can be cooked or eaten raw when young in salads.

plants (3 seeds per module) in beds, 22cm (8½in) between plants, 22cm (8½in) between rows. Protect from flea beetle (see page 82). Salad rocket bolts quickly in late spring, providing pretty flowers for pollinators. Suitable as a baby-leaf crop on a windowsill (see Pots, page 152).

CHICORY

Has bitter leaves. Can be grown large to harvest the bitter hearts, or as a cut-and-come-again baby leaves. For baby leaves direct sow in late July to early August, spacing 10cm (4in) between plants, 30cm (12in) between rows. In pots, 15cm (6in) between seedlings will yield good-sized leaves for salads. Snip leaves from around the outside of plants, leaving the central growing point intact to keep producing. Use any mix of chicory varieties for a cut-and-come-again crop, including 'Castelfranco', 'Palla Rossa', 'Grumolo Verde', 'Sugarloaf' and 'Treviso'.

← A single lettuce 'Little Gem' in a pot, ideal for a small space.

COMMON PROBLEMS

Slugs (see Pests, page 80). Pick leaves regularly to prevent hiding places.

Lettuce root aphid (see page 80).

Downy mildew (see Diseases, page 84).

POTS

Pot size: Minimum depth 10cm (4in), minimum diameter 15cm (6in).

Indoor windowsills: Yes (baby leaf or one lettuce head per pot).

Shallow-rooting salad is the perfect crop for pots.

Baby leaf will grow in narrower diameter pots (e.g. a recycled tin can) but yields will be less plentiful. Conversely lettuce heads need a wider diameter. The Charles Dowding method (see page 146–7) can be used in containers, provided they're big enough. Aim for a 35–45cm (14–18in) diameter pot. You can plant a little closer than 22cm (8½in) between plants, 22cm (8½in) between rows, but keep picking regularly. Leaves may be smaller than in open ground.

For very small spaces, see Microgreens, page 28, or try baby-leaf lettuce in small pots and window boxes (ready-made seed mixes are available, or see More salad leaves, pages 148–51).

BABY LEAF SALAD SOWING

Fill a wide, shallow pot or tray with organic, peat-free multipurpose compost. Firm down the compost to create a flat surface using your hand or a piece of wood. Moisten and sprinkle seeds over the surface. Cover lightly with 5mm (around ⅛in) of compost. Water well.

Once germinated, thin the seedlings to 2cm (¾in) apart.

Feed pots with organic liquid/homemade feed every 2 weeks (see page 36).

Your first harvest will be in 3–4 weeks. Snip a few small leaves from around each plant, using a sharp knife to harvest. This gives far better regrowth than cutting across the whole patch with scissors.

Sow every 2–3 weeks for a constant supply, rotating between a few pots. Resow into the first pot once harvested – simply replenish with 1cm (¼in) of fresh potting compost and start again.

Recipe
Summer garden salad

Ingredients per person

Lettuce leaves
(2 handfuls)

Flavour leaves
(1 handful)

Herbs
(½ handful)

Flowers
(½ handful)

For the dressing (serves 4)

6 tablespoons olive oil

2 tablespoons red wine vinegar or apple cider vinegar

1 teaspoon Dijon mustard

½ lemon

Sea salt flakes

→ A joyful basket of mixed salad leaves and edible flowers.

Many of the leaves in this salad don't transport well and are rarely found in the shops. They are a joy to gather fresh and to eat soon after.

Build your salad...

TEXTURE

Use crunchy lettuce as your base (see page 147 for varieties). Add summer purslane, New Zealand spinach and pea shoots for a plump, juicy bite.

FLAVOUR

Add pops of sour and heat for punch. Sour: sorrel (and oxalis if you have it as a weed, see page 87). Heat: microgreens – rocket, red mustard, Greek cress.

UP THE FLAVOUR

Choose your chopped herbs: basil, chives, parsley, tarragon, mint.

COLOUR

Finish with edible flowers: viola, calendula, nasturtium, French marigold.

DRESSING

Mix 3 parts olive oil and 1 part red wine or apple cider vinegar with the Dijon mustard and lemon juice and a pinch of sea salt flakes.

Tomatoes

I started my vegetable growing career at Buttervilla Farm on the south coast of Cornwall. Owners Robert and Gill grew the best tomatoes I'd ever eaten – sharp, sweet, juicy – the essence of summer. The exceptional flavour came from carefully selected heritage varieties, good 'muck', added warmth from the polytunnels and a tendency not to overwater or overfeed. Tomatoes are more abundant inside a greenhouse in UK summers. However, the right outdoor varieties (see below) still offer delicious rewards.

Growing tips

* Tomatoes grow as vines or bushes – check seed catalogue descriptions. Vines (also known as cordons or indeterminate types) grow tall and require training up a support and pinching out (see page 156) to maintain one central stem. Bush types (also known as indeterminate) can be left alone. There are also varieties bred specifically for pots – these are more compact, or trailing for hanging baskets.
* Choose early fruiting varieties for outdoor growing. Early bush types or cherry tomatoes work well. Ensure plants are in a sunny, sheltered spot. Positioning pots against south-facing walls or fences is best.
* For indoor plants, keep spaces well ventilated – by late June I leave my greenhouse doors open day and night. Damp down the floor on hot days, being careful not to touch the foliage with water.
* A healthy, well-composted/manured soil (done in winter prior to planting) has always supported my plants without the need to feed, despite talk of high potash tomato feed being necessary. A homemade nettle or comfrey feed is a nice tonic (see page 70), especially for plants grown in containers (see Pots, page 158).
* Keep plants consistently moist but do not overwater, especially when young. My plants growing in soil in the greenhouse are watered every 3 days on average. Less watering later in the season will lead to sweeter fruit, but does limit yield. See also Pots, page 158.
* Pinch out sideshoots (see page 156).
* Tomatoes are great planting companions with basil and French marigolds.

SOWING/PLANTING

Sow indoors in modules from February to early April.

My preferred sowing date is late February for tomatoes that will be grown in a greenhouse. Do not sow these later than mid-March.

For outdoor growing, sow indoors in modules a little later in March or early April.

→ Trusses of the ever-popular 'Gardener's Delight' tomato.

Sow 2 seeds per module, thinning to 1 once germinated. Cover the seeds with compost.

Tomatoes prefer warm temperatures for germination (16–30°C/61–86°F). This can take a few weeks, so be patient.

Modules will need potting on into 9cm (3½in) pots before planting in their final destination (see Potting on, page 66).

Harden off plants to be planted outdoors (see Hardening off, page 66).

Tomatoes can form roots along their stems, so burying them deep (up to the first or even second set of leaves) when potting on and planting out will create a better rooting system. If stems are long, you can lay them flat to the side of the planting hole.

↑ Tie a tomato stem to its support with string in a figure-of-eight knot.

↑ Pinch out tomato sideshoots between your fingers or use secateurs, to make the plant more productive.

SUPPORT

For my greenhouse 'cordon' plants, I use canes/sticks as supports – running a taut wire attached to the greenhouse walls horizontally along the top of the canes adds stability. As they grow, keep tying the tomato stems into the canes with string using a figure-of-eight knot. You can also hang strings loosely from the greenhouse roof and bury the ends under the rootballs of the tomatoes at planting time. You need enough slack to then carefully twist the stem of the tomato around the string as it grows to support it.

Sturdy supports are needed outside; if growing plants in a row of pots, brace any upright canes with horizontals sticks or wires.

Depending on how unruly your bush tomato is, you may wish to use a stake to prop it up, but generally bush tomatoes can be left without supports.

PINCHING OUT

As cordon plants grow upwards, new sideshoots will form between the leaves and the stem. These need removing or the plant will become less productive, with more energy going into leaf production than fruits. When small, they can be rubbed off between your fingers (giving you genuinely green fingers) or you can snip them off with secateurs.

This is ongoing throughout the season. In late summer, once plants have formed 4–5 trusses outside, and 6–7 trusses inside, pinch out the main growing point 2 leaves above the top truss. This aids ripening.

Bush types don't need pinching out.

Earlier in the season, sideshoots can be used to make more plants if needed. Simply stand in a glass of water until they form roots and then pot up.

Keep removing yellowing bottom sets of leaves to aid air circulation. I remove at least the first 30cm (12in) of bottom leaves, if not more, for good airflow (even if they're still green).

SPACINGS
(FOR POTS, SEE PAGE 158)

Outdoors: space plants 45cm (18in) apart.

Indoors: leave 50cm (20in) between plants, 75cm (30in) between rows for better ventilation.

Plant in single rows or staggered double rows.

Allow 45cm (18in) between outside plants grown in pots or in a grow bag. Don't cluster plants together, as this can lead to blight.

↓ Grow a mix of tomato varieties to yield a beautiful array of colours, shapes and sizes.

HARVESTING

Pick fruits as they ripen. If the last trusses haven't ripened before frost is due in autumn, make green tomato chutney (see recipe on page 159).

VARIETIES

'Brad's Atomic Grape', 'Berner Rose', 'Black Cherry', 'Chocolate Cherry', 'Gardener's Delight', 'Green Zebra', 'Stupice', 'Paul Robeson', 'Pink Tiger', 'Marmande', 'Yellow Submarine', 'Roma', 'Costoluto Fiorentino', 'Sungold' F1.

Perform well outdoors: 'Gardener's Delight', 'Latah', 'Stupice', 'Chadwick Cherry', 'Alicante', 'Sungold' F1 and any of the smaller cherry types above.

Hanging baskets and pots: 'Tumbling Tom' (red and yellow), 'Losetto', 'Cherry Cascade' (F1 varieties).

Windowsill: 'Micro Tom', 'Orange Hat', 'Red Robin', 'Totem' (F1 varieties), 'House Tomato'.

DESIGN TIPS

Grow with purple basil and French marigolds.

← Outdoor tomatoes need plenty of sunshine. This pot stands against a south-facing wall, to maximize the amount of warmth it receives.

Fill containers with organic, peat-free, multipurpose potting compost.

Only ever plant 1 tomato per pot or hanging basket.

Underplant pots (not hanging baskets) with 1 basil and 1 French marigold but keep well watered to support all three.

If available, top-dress with garden or worm compost.

Organic, peat-free grow bags can be used – plant only 2 tomatoes per bag. Stack one bag on top of the other for more rooting depth (see page 33).

Start feeding after the first yellow flowers form with organic liquid/homemade comfrey feed every 2 weeks (see page 36).

Hanging baskets will need daily watering. I use sheep's wool to insulate mine, which retains water and keeps the compost cool. Coir liners are also available.

COMMON PROBLEMS

Tomatoes are susceptible to attacks from blight, blossom end rot, whitefly and red spider mite (see pages 80–85.

Fruit splitting, caused by irregular watering: water consistently.

POTS

Pot size: Minimum depth 30cm (12in); minimum diameter 35cm (14in).

Indoor windowsill: Yes (see Varieties, page 157).

There is a tomato for every size of plot, from hanging baskets to windowsills.

Follow previous information for growing tips, sowing and planting in pots.

Recipe
Tomato & apple chutney

Ingredients for 6–7 jars (depending on size)

1.5kg (3lb 5oz) tomatoes (green, red or a mix), roughly chopped

400g (14oz) onions, diced

3 eating or cooking apples, peeled, cored and diced

3 garlic cloves, finely chopped

2 red chillies, deseeded and diced, or 2 teaspoons dried chilli flakes

Large knob of fresh ginger, peeled and grated

200g (7oz) sultanas

250g (8oz) soft light brown sugar

1 teaspoon salt

500ml (18fl oz) apple cider vinegar

To sterilize the jars, wash in warm soapy water, rinse and allow to air dry. Place in the oven at 150°C/300°F/ Gas 2 for 15 minutes. Choose plastic-coated lids (vinegar will react with metal) and boil for 10 minutes to sterilize.

Everyone needs a green tomato chutney recipe up their sleeve, especially in climates where later fruits can fail to ripen. Autumn chutney-making coincides with apple season, and the two are obvious bedfellows. This recipe also works with red tomatoes, or a mix of red and green.

Place all the ingredients, except the vinegar, in a large preserving or heavy-based saucepan. Pour over three-quarters of the vinegar. Bring to the boil, then reduce the heat and simmer uncovered for 2–3 hours or until the mixture is thick and reduced. Stir occasionally to prevent it sticking to the pan and add the remaining vinegar if it needs more liquid, until a good chutney consistency is reached.

While the mixture is still warm, spoon into the sterilized jars and seal with the lids. Invert the jars and allow to stand for 10 minutes to allow the chutney to sterilize the lids, before turning the right way up. Leave in a cool, dark place for a few weeks or up to a year for the flavours to develop. Once opened, keep in the fridge and use within 4 weeks.

Winter squash

Winter squashes are endlessly enchanting. As their foliage fades in autumn, brilliant flashes of orange, blue, red and yellow glow against heavy skies. Pumpkins and winter squashes are part of the same family, but squashes have a superior flavour that is sweet and caramel-like when roasted. That said, the smallest pumpkin, 'Jack-Be-Little', is utterly delicious. For pots and small spaces, pick smaller-fruiting varieties to train up supports. Unlike their summer siblings, winter squashes store well, meaning you can enjoy them well into winter. Their curious colours and shapes look lovely adorning the shelves in your home, until you're ready to devour them.

Growing tips

* Winter squashes enjoy plenty of sunshine.
* Plants are killed by frost.
* They are hungry plants. Ensure you've spread compost or well-rotted manure in the winter prior to planting. And an extra helping in planting holes won't go amiss.
* Plants grown along the ground root at various points on the stem, taking up more water and nutrients. Growing the plants upwards and in pots doesn't allow this, so they need feeding (see page 36).
* Keep well watered, especially plants in pots and on supports.
* If training up, tie squash stems loosely onto the framework with string or twine – they will send out tendrils to grab on with. See Grow up, page 72, for plant support ideas. Frameworks can be as simple as wires secured along a fence or a tepee wrapped with string (see 'Tromboncino', page 126). Just ensure that what you use is sturdy, as the plants will be heavier once the fruits swell.
* If growing larger fruiting types up, you will need to support the fruit once it starts to swell, so that the plant doesn't buckle under the weight. Using an old pair of tights as a cradle works well.

SOWING/PLANTING

Sow from April to May.

Sow indoors in 9cm (3½in) pots (or similar) in mid-April. They like warmer temperatures for germination, ideally 21–35°C (70–95°F).

Make a hole 1–2cm (¼–¾in) deep, drop in the seed and cover with compost. Sow 2 seeds per pot to ensure germination, and thin to the strongest seedling once established.

← A 'Jack-Be-Little' pumpkin growing with a trailing nasturtium.

Alternatively, direct sow outdoors from mid- to late May. Sow 2–3 seeds per station (3cm/1in deep) and thin to the strongest seedling once established. Direct sown plants won't be as productive as those sown earlier indoors.

Don't be tempted to sow too early (earlier than mid-April indoors), as you'll be battling the cold. Similarly, don't sow/plant outside until the last frost has passed in mid- to late May (UK).

If your plant outgrows its pot, don't be tempted to place it outside too early. Pot it on to a larger pot before planting out in its final destination.

Harden off plants (see page 66) and cover with fleece after planting outside for quicker establishment.

← Winter squash: 'Ute Indian', 'Delicata', 'Sweet Dumpling'; pumpkin: 'Jack-Be-Little'; summer squash (dried): 'Tromboncino'.

CURING

Curing intensifies the sweetness and hardens the skins, meaning that fruits will last longer when stored over winter.

To cure, simply place them somewhere warm with good airflow for a few weeks. Then store them somewhere cool, frost-free and dry until needed. However, most of us don't have this type of space, plus, they're too pretty to hide away! I have them dotted around my kitchen and they keep fine.

VARIETIES

Smaller-fruiting varieties for training upwards in small spaces: 'Jack-Be-Little' pumpkin, 'Delicata', 'Sweet Dumpling', 'Uchiki Kuri'/'Orange Hokkaido'/'Red Kuri', 'Thelma Sanders', 'Sweet Potato' (acorn squash), 'Tuffy'.

Larger, great-tasting fruit: 'Ute Indian', 'Black Futsu'.

SPACINGS
(FOR POTS, SEE OPPOSITE)

You need a lot of space for a pumpkin/squash patch in open ground – plants require 90cm (3ft) between plants and 1.5m (5ft) between rows. That's why training up a trellis or support saves on space, whether it is in containers or beds. Space plants 75cm (2½ft) apart if growing in a row along a wall, fence or trellis. This frees up the rest of the bed for an understorey of herbs, edible flowers or salads.

HARVESTING

Fruit ripens in autumn; October is the main harvest month.

Pick before the frost arrives.

Give the fruit a tap – it should sound hollow if it is ripe.

Be careful not to snap off the stem when harvesting, as the fruit may then rot at the base. For good storage, keep the stem as long as possible, and don't carry squashes around by the stem.

↓ The small-fruiting 'Delicata' squash can be trained upwards on a support as well as grown trailing on the ground.

Try 'Rouge Vif d'Etampes' for a reasonably flavoured Cinderella pumpkin at Halloween.

DESIGN TIPS

Grow well with nasturtiums, which draw in pollinators for optimum fruiting.

COMMON PROBLEMS

Generally problem-free.

Slugs (see page 79).

Powdery mildew (see page 84).

POTS

Pot size: Minimum depth 45cm (18in); minimum diameter 50cm (20in).

Indoor windowsill: No.

Use as large a pot as you can accommodate or a trough/old bathtub – the bigger the better.

Fill containers with organic, peat-free, multipurpose potting compost.

Winter squashes like to spread their roots. Only ever plant 1 plant per pot.

If available, top-dress with garden or worm compost to provide extra nutrients and conserve moisture.

Stand in a sunny spot, keep well watered and feed pots with organic liquid/homemade feed every 2 weeks (see page 36).

Herb spotlights

My first herb garden took shape on a windswept windowledge on the Cornish coast in 2005. Since then I've kept this hotchpotch of potted plants close – they've accompanied me, via various gardens and stages of life, their offspring now in residence in Suffolk. I see herbs as non-negotiables, essential to my cooking and allies in supporting my wellbeing. They also perform a crucial role attracting pollinators and beneficial insects. Perfect small-space plants, there is a herb for most aspects.

POINTERS

✱ A 5-litre (1⅓-gallon) pot (22cm/9in diameter) generally works well for growing single herbs outside, but I've given minimum measurements if small spaces don't allow for this. Keep potting on herbs for larger plants. The queen of herbs Jekka McVicar advises to only pot herbs up one size at a time. Don't take a little herb and put it in a big pot, as this can slow growth or even kill the plant. Move it on gradually, and always use crocks for drainage.

✱ Herbs can be mixed in pots and window boxes but ensure they have the same watering needs. Group Mediterranean herbs together, and don't mix with those that enjoy damp conditions, like chives, chervil, mint and parsley. (See individual plant profiles for watering needs.)

✱ I've noted which herbs suit windowsill growing. If your sill gets 6 hours of sun a day, then it should be able to raise healthy herbs. Opt for chives, mint and parsley on shadier sills.

→ Edible thyme flowers with aromatic rosemary and sage.

Basil

This sun-loving herb offers a wonderful range of varieties. All are best friends with tomatoes (especially sweet basil), but also try Thai basil in Asian dishes, lemon basil in salads and cinnamon basil and holy basil in tea.

Growing tips

* Annual.
* Performs best in a greenhouse or sunny conservatory. If growing outside, position in a warm, sheltered spot.
* Young seedlings hate sitting in damp compost overnight – water in the morning and sparingly, as they are prone to damping off (see page 83).
* Keep well watered once you have established plants.
* Cut back the flowers as they appear, to keep the plant producing leaves.
* Basil and tomatoes grow well together.

→ Purple basil looks beautiful growing in a container.

SOWING/PLANTING

Sow indoors in modules from April to June. They prefer a temperature of 20–25°C (68–77°F) to germinate. Lightly cover the seed with compost.

Thin to 1 seedling per module once germinated.

Don't plant outside until all danger of frost has passed. This may mean plants need potting on before they go outside.

Harden off first (see page 66).

SPACINGS
(FOR POTS, SEE BELOW)

Leave 25cm (10in) between plants, 25cm (10in) between rows.

COMMON PROBLEMS

Can be susceptible to damping off (see page 83) and whitefly (see page 81).

← Cinnamon basil has a cinnamon-like flavour as well as scent.

HARVESTING

Pinch out the growing tips (from the top) to keep plants bushy.

Plants will slow down by mid-autumn and are killed by the first frosts.

VARIETIES

'Sweet Genovese', cinnamon basil, sweet basil, Thai basil, purple basil, lime basil, lemon basil, Greek basil, bush basil, holy basil (tulsi) – wonderful in tea but needs to be grown indoors.

DESIGN TIPS

Purple and cinnamon basil make beautiful additions to pots and hanging baskets.

POTS

Pot size: Minimum depth 15cm (6in); minimum diameter 20cm (8in) – choose bigger pots for mixed plantings.

Indoor windowsill: Yes – 1-litre (1¾ pint) pots, 11cm (4in) deep × 13cm (5in) in diameter.

Fill containers with organic, peat-free, multipurpose potting compost.

I find 3 plants to a 35cm (14in) diameter pot is very productive (standing in a sunny spot).

Feed with organic liquid/homemade feed every 2 weeks (see page 36).

Chervil

Raymond Blanc eagerly introduced me to chervil. Used widely in France, its delicate, fern-like leaves taste of aniseed and add a touch of elegance to everyday dishes. Particularly good with a simple omelette.

Growing tips

* Annual.
* Likes cool, damp conditions. Is likely to bolt in summer.
* Hardy herb best grown for spring/autumn/winter use.
* Allow to flower in spring and it will self-set around your plot.

SOWING/PLANTING

Sow indoors in modules in late July/August for autumn pickings. Cover the seed with compost. Plants should overwinter for another harvest in March/April.

Thin to 3 seedlings per module, planting out as a clump once they are established.

Alternatively, direct sow in drills outdoors (see page 68) in late July or August.

SPACINGS
(FOR POTS, SEE BELOW)

Space modules 20cm (8 in) apart. For direct-sown drills leave 10cm (4in) between plants and 20cm (8in) between rows.

HARVESTING

Pick outer leaves from around the base of the plant.

VARIETIES

I prefer ordinary chervil, as opposed to curly leaved.

DESIGN TIPS

The lacy foliage looks pretty in winter window boxes.

COMMON PROBLEMS

Bolts in summer heat, so follow the sowing dates.

↑ A young chervil plant.

POTS

Minimum depth: 15cm (6in); minimum diameter 20cm (8in).

Indoor windowsill: No.

Fill pots and containers with organic, peat-free, multipurpose potting compost.

If sowing direct, firm down the compost to create a flat surface using your hand or a piece of wood. Scatter seeds thinly on top, covering lightly with a 2cm (¾in) layer of compost. Water well. Once germinated, thin to 15cm (6in) apart in all directions.

Keep compost damp but not wet.

Feed with organic liquid/homemade feed every 2 weeks (see page 36).

Chives

↑ White-flowered garlic chives.

Grow two types: common chives with purple pompom flowers, and white-flowered garlic chives with a sweet garlic flavour. Both varieties make beautiful edging plants, adored by pollinators.

Growing tips

* Perennial.
* Deadhead flowers as they fade.
* Happy in sun but will tolerate semi-shade.
* Keep plants moist.
* Divide plants every 3 years. Lift with a fork and separate little clumps of 10 bulbs to replant.

SOWING/PLANTING

Sow seeds indoors in modules in March.

Sow 10–15 seeds per module to a depth of 1cm (¼in). Cover with compost.

Wait until frost has passed before planting out as a clump.

Alternatively, for ease, buy plants (see Resources, pages 220–1).

SPACINGS
(FOR POTS, SEE BELOW)

Space plants 15cm (6in) apart, or 10cm (4in) apart for edging.

COMMON PROBLEMS

Rust (bright yellow/orange spots on leaves). Cut back immediately. Keep the soil moist.

HARVESTING

Cut leaves back to 3cm (1in) above ground level.

Flowers and flower buds are also edible – break the flower heads apart and scatter individual florets over dishes.

VARIETIES

Chives (purple flowers), garlic chives (white flowers).

DESIGN TIPS

Grow as a pretty edging (see Spacings, above) or around carrot pots, to deter carrot fly.

POTS

Pot size: Minimum depth 10cm (4in); minimum diameter 13cm (5in) – deeper is better.

Indoor windowsill: Yes – tolerates semi-shade, use 1-litre (1¾ pint) pots, 11cm (4in) deep and 13cm (5in) in diameter.

Fill containers with organic, peat-free, multipurpose potting compost.

Keep container chives well watered. Place in semi-shade so they don't dry out.

Feed with organic liquid/homemade feed every 3–4 weeks (see page 36).

Lemon verbena

An essential plant for appreciators of herbal teas. The heavenly scent of lemon sherbet fizzes from this plant, making a delicious (surprisingly calming) digestif tea (see recipe opposite). Infuse into ice cream and sorbets; flavour oils and syrups; or simply stroke to lift your mood.

Growing tips

↑ Harvesting sprigs of lemon verbena.

* Half-hardy perennial.
* Sun-loving.
* Needs winter protection. Bring pots into a frost-free, cool place (porch or cold greenhouse) or raise them off the ground, mulch the roots well with compost and cover with fleece. In beds, either lift the plants, pot up and move indoors, as above, or mulch and cover with fleece in situ. If you are in a particularly cold part of the country, bring plants indoors. Keep compost on the dry side over winter.

* Plants drop leaves and go dormant in winter. They reshoot in spring very slowly; plants may look dead but don't give up on them. Scratch the bark with a fingernail and if it's still green beneath, it's alive!
* Once it starts shooting in spring, cut out any dead or damaged branches and cut back last year's growth to 4cm (1½in).
* Produces pretty lilac flowers in summer – trim back lightly after flowering.

SOWING/PLANTING

For ease, buy plants (see Resources, pages 220–1).

Plant outside when danger of frost has passed.

SPACINGS
(FOR POTS, SEE OPPOSITE)

45cm (18in) between plants, 45cm (18in) between rows.

DESIGN TIPS

Looks elegant in a large pot.

Recipe
Lemon verbena iced tea

HARVESTING

Harvest sprigs as needed. Leaves can be dried for winter use.

COMMON PROBLEMS

Killed by hard winters
(see opposite).

POTS

Pot size: Minimum depth 20cm (8in); minimum diameter 20cm (8in), a bigger pot equals a bigger plant.

Indoor windowsill: No.

Fill containers with organic, peat-free, multipurpose potting compost and plant 1 plant per pot.

Plants in pots need a sunny, sheltered spot to thrive.

Needs winter protection – see Growing tips, opposite.

Keep well watered and feed with organic liquid/homemade feed during flowering (see page 36).

Ingredients

1 large handful of lemon verbena sprigs (or 50:50 mix of verbena and mint)

2 teaspoons honey or rose geranium syrup (see page 211), both optional

Lemon slices, to garnish

Ice cubes or edible flower ice cubes (see page 217)

Bring 1 litre (1¾ pints) water *almost* to the boil in a saucepan.

Remove from the heat and add the lemon verbena. Add the honey to taste or rose geranium syrup if you prefer sweeter tea, cover and leave to steep for 10 minutes.

Strain into a jug and refrigerate until chilled. For a stronger infusion, leave the herbs in and steep overnight in the fridge (then strain before serving).

Serve over ice with lemon slices and edible flower ice cubes. Garnish with verbena and mint.

Lemon verbena tea is delicious warm or chilled. On a hot summer's day served ice cold, it is beautifully refreshing. This recipe also works well with the addition of mint.

Mint

↑ Apple mint, delicious in apple jelly.

Fresh mint is integral to spring and summer kitchens; use liberally with new potatoes, courgettes, strawberries, in mint tea and mojitos! Whatever your tipple, there are many charming mint varieties to choose from.

Growing tips

* Perennial.
* Plant in sun or semi-shade.
* Keep well watered.
* Mint is also a thug – best grown in pots to stop the roots spreading. In beds, plant in bottomless pots (30cm/12in depth), leaving the rim just protruding above soil level.
* Edible flowers attract beneficial insects. Cut plants back to 5–10cm (2–4in) above the soil after flowering to encourage new growth.
* Don't grow different varieties next to each other, as their scents/flavours will lose their potency.

SOWING/PLANTING

Seed is not worthwhile, so buy plants (see Resources, pages 220–1), divide or take cuttings (see method opposite).

IN DEPTH: DIVIDING MINT

Container plants need dividing every 2 years, as the roots wrap around the inside of pots limiting growth. If the growth looks bare in the middle, it's time. In spring, upturn the pot, remove the rootball and divide in half or quarters (depending on size) with a sharp spade or trowel. No need to be gentle. Replant sections to make new plants.

SPACINGS
(FOR POTS, SEE OPPOSITE)

Plant 30cm (12in) apart.

HARVESTING

Pick from spring to autumn from the top down. The plants die back in winter.

COMMON PROBLEMS

Rust (bright yellow/orange spots on leaves). Cut back immediately. Keep the soil moist.

Mint cuttings
(Spring/Summer)

You can even make new plants with mint bought in a packet from a supermarket.

DESIGN TIPS

Apple mint has particularly pretty flowers and foliage.

VARIETIES

Spearmint (all rounder), Moroccan mint and peppermint (for tea), apple mint (for desserts and jellies).

Other fun scents: ginger, strawberry, chocolate, pineapple, eau de Cologne.

POTS

Pot size: Minimum depth 15cm (6in); minimum diameter 20cm (8in).

Indoor windowsill: Yes – tolerates semi-shade. Use 1-litre (1¾ pint) pots, 11cm (4in) deep and 13cm (5in) in diameter.

Fill containers with organic, peat-free, multipurpose potting compost. Only 1 variety per pot. Place in semi-shade and keep well watered, do not allow to dry out. Feed fortnightly.

1 With a sharp knife or scissors, cut a 10cm (4in) long cutting from the top growth of the plant and remove the lower leaves.

2 With a sharp knife, cut the stem just below a leaf node (these are the little raised lines from where leaves emerge).

3 Place stems in a glass of water. Stand on a light windowsill (but not in full sun) until the stems take root – usually 2–3 weeks. Replenish the water every 3–4 days.

4 Once a good root system develops, pot on into individual pots and keep well watered. These plants (pictured) have a bit further to go before roots establish.

Parsley

Parsley is so much more than a limp garnish. Homegrown, it tastes crisp, sweet and full of vitality. Containing more iron than spinach, and full of essential vitamins, minerals and antioxidants, parsley packs a nutritional punch.

Growing tips

* Hardy biennial.
* Enjoys a damp, semi-shaded spot in summer. Keep consistently moist.
* For overwintering plants (sown in July), choose a sunny, sheltered spot. Plants can survive winter in milder areas, to give spring leaves before flowering.
* For guaranteed winter supplies, sow in pots in July and bring onto the windowsill in autumn.
* Hungry plant; needs fertile soil and regular liquid feeds when grown in pots.

SOWING/PLANTING

Sow flat-leaved parsley in March *and* July (for supplies into winter).

Sow indoors in modules. Cover seeds lightly with compost.

Thin to 1 seedling per module.

Alternatively, sow direct. Make a drill (see page 68).

Parsley is slow to germinate.

Cover early sowings/plantings with fleece.

SPACINGS
(FOR POTS, SEE RIGHT)

Space modules 15cm (6in) between plants, 22cm (8½in) between rows.

Thin seedlings in direct-sown drills to 2–3cm (¾–1in) apart.

HARVESTING

Pick whole stems from the bottom of the plant for a continuous supply.

VARIETIES

Flat-leaved types have a better flavour, than curled (in my opinion).

DESIGN TIPS

Allow a few plants to flower in their second year, when the beautiful white umbels will attract beneficial insects.

COMMON PROBLEMS

Slugs (see page 79).

Carrot fly (see page 80) – a barrier is not usually needed. Resow the crop if plants are badly affected.

POTS

Pot size: Minimum depth 20cm (8in); minimum diameter 20cm (8in). Parsley has a large tap root so use the deepest pot you can fit.

Indoor windowsill: Yes – tolerates semi-shade,

Fill pots and containers with organic, peat-free, multipurpose potting compost.

Smaller pots: 1 plant per pot.

Larger pots: 4 plants in a 30cm (12in) pot.

Place in semi-shade.

Keep well watered, do not allow to dry out and feed with organic liquid/homemade feed every 2 weeks (see page 36).

← Flat-leaved parsley – my desert island kitchen herb.

Recipe
Parsley & rosemary pesto

Ingredients

1 handful pumpkin and
sunflower seeds
(50:50 mix of each)

½ garlic clove

1 big bunch of parsley

3 sprigs of rosemary

Extra virgin olive oil

Big handful of freshly
grated Parmesan cheese
(optional)

Juice of ½ lemon

Sea salt flakes and
black pepper

My friend Maya introduced me to this pesto – a nourishing accompaniment to soups, vegetables and pasta. Pesto is a lovely way of adding more herbs to your diet. This recipe is also delicious without the cheese – just add a little more salt. A pestle and mortar yields a better flavour, but for bigger batches a food processor is handy – just pop all the ingredients in the blender and mix.

1 Toast the seeds lightly in a dry frying pan for a few minutes over a medium heat. Set aside to cool.

2 Meanwhile, crush the garlic with a pinch of sea salt flakes using a pestle and mortar.

3 Pick the leaves from the stems of the herbs, roughly chop the parsley and finely chop the rosemary. Add the herbs and toasted seeds to the garlic and pound together.

4 Add a good glug of olive oil to create a sauce.

5 Add the cheese (if using) and the lemon juice. Taste and season with salt and pepper. Add more cheese, oil or lemon to taste until you're happy.

Rosemary

↓ The pretty blue flowers of rosemary are edible, with a delicious rosemary punch.

Rosemary has long been used as a 'head' herb, stimulating blood flow to the brain and improving concentration and memory. Students in Ancient Greece wore wreaths of rosemary during their exams; I may resort to that to finish this book…or simply put sprigs in my water bottle and my bath (see page 179)!

Growing tips

* Hardy perennial.
* Needs well-drained soil and a sunny spot – it's a Mediterranean herb.
* Don't overwater.
* In cold areas, young plants need winter protection – use fleece, mulch the roots with compost and grow by a sunny wall.
* Trim back after flowering in spring. The flowers are edible and popular with bees.
* For old, straggly plants, cut back hard in spring.

SOWING/PLANTING

For ease and quicker establishment, buy plants (see Resources, pages 220–1).

SPACINGS
(FOR POTS, SEE RIGHT)

Plant 60cm (2ft) apart.

COMMON PROBLEMS

Rosemary beetle, a striking, metallic beetle, and its larvae eat the leaves. Pick them off young plants if you spot them. Doesn't tend to affect the overall health of established plants.

HARVESTING

Pick leaves year-round but go easy in winter.

VARIETIES

'Miss Jessopp's Upright', 'Jekka's Blue', 'Majorca Pink', 'Foxtail', 'Green Ginger' (great for cocktails), any prostrate (trailing) rosemary.

DESIGN TIPS

Grow prostrate varieties to trail over pots and walls.

Grows well as a hedge, with plants 45cm (18in) apart. Try 'Miss Jessopp's Upright'.

POTS

Pot size: Minimum depth 20cm (8in); minimum diameter 20cm (8in), bigger is better.

Indoor windowsill: No – can survive on a windowsill but won't thrive.

The bigger the pot, the bigger the plant.

Fill containers with organic, peat-free, multipurpose potting compost.

1 plant per pot.

Ensure the compost is well drained, don't overwater, but water well in dry spells.

Feed with organic liquid/homemade feed only after flowering (see page 36).

Recipe
Rosemary bath salts

**Ingredients for
3 baths**

3 cupfuls of magnesium/
Epsom salts

½ cupful of fresh rosemary
leaves (picked from stems
and roughly chopped)

1 tablespoon organic
sunflower or olive oil

20 drops of lavender
essential oil

You will also need a piece of
muslin 30 x 30cm (12 x 12in),
and jute string

*Note: Essential oils can make
the bath slippery, so take care.
Rosemary can also leave a tea-
stain mark in the bath, but it
easily cleans off! This mixture
is best used fresh, so use within
a few weeks.*

*Warm water, homegrown herbs, mineral salts and therapeutic
oils are a recipe for relaxation. Rosemary is invigorating and
can ease aching muscles. Also experiment with other fresh herbs
such as calendula, mint and lemon verbena.*

1 Mix the salts and rosemary
together in a blender or
food processor.

2 Transfer to a bowl and stir in the
sunflower oil and essential oil.

3 Store in an airtight glass jar.

4 To use, place a cupful of the
mix in the centre of the piece
of muslin, gather together the sides
and tie with a long piece of string.

5 Hang the muslin pouch over
the tap, or hold under the water
stream while the bath is running,
to dissolve the mixture. If the
mixture is added to the bathtub
without being in the muslin, the
herbs may clog the plughole.

6 Once you're in the bathtub,
relax and soak for 20 minutes
minimum! The muslin pouch can
be left to float around like a teabag.

Sage

Once regarded as a panacea for every disease, sage's botanical name *Salvia* is derived from the Latin *salvare*, meaning 'to save'. The antibacterial and antiviral properties of common sage make it a helpful ally in the cold and flu season. I add a sprig of it to a honey and lemon infusion for soothing a sore throat, and to my winter oxymel recipe (see page 187).

← Pineapple sage is a great addition to cocktails and fruit salads.

Growing tips

* Hardy perennial.
* A Mediterranean herb that needs well-drained soil and a sunny spot.
* Don't overwater.
* In cold areas, young plants need winter protection – cover with fleece, mulch the roots with compost and grow by a sunny wall.
* Cut mature plants back hard in spring, and trim back again after flowering.
* The beautiful edible flowers attract pollinators and beneficial insects.

SOWING/PLANTING

For ease and quicker establishment, buy plants (see Resources, pages 220–1).

SPACINGS
(FOR POTS, SEE OPPOSITE)

Leave 45cm (18in) between plants, 45cm (18in) between rows.

HARVESTING

Pick leaves year-round but go easy in winter.

VARIETIES

Common sage, purple/red sage.

Pineapple sage, blackcurrant sage (pretty edible flowers with scented leaves, as their names suggest; neither is hardy, so bring indoors for winter).

DESIGN TIPS

Pineapple sage is spectacular in a large container.

→ Common sage in flower is a wonderful lure for pollinators.

COMMON PROBLEMS

Becomes woody over time, so may need replacing every 4–5 years.

Plants sometimes die without warning, usually in wet winters or if overwatered. Replace.

POTS

Pot size: Minimum depth 20cm (8in); minimum diameter 20cm (8in). The bigger the pot, the bigger the plant. Pineapple sage benefits from a large pot.

Windowsill: No (hates windowsills).

Fill containers with organic, peat-free, multipurpose potting compost.

Ensure the compost is well drained; don't overwater but water well in dry spells.

Feed with organic liquid/ homemade feed only after flowering (see page 36).

French tarragon

A classic herb of French cuisine with dainty, aniseed-flavoured leaves. Aside from its traditional pairing with chicken and as an ingredient in béarnaise sauce, it works surprisingly well with strawberries, oysters, eggs and asparagus. Tarragon vinegar is a delight in salad dressings.

Growing tips

* Grow French, not Russian, tarragon (Russian tarragon lacks flavour).
* Enjoys a warm, sunny spot.
* Don't overwater.
* Remove flowers in summer.
* The plant goes dormant in winter and the foliage dies back.
* Needs protection in winter. Before first frosts, mulch around the base and cover the plant with fleece.

SOWING/PLANTING

French tarragon cannot be raised from seed. Buy plants (see Resources, pages 220–1).

Plants need replacing every 3 years for the best flavour.

SPACING
(FOR POTS, SEE OPPOSITE)

Leave 60cm (2ft) between plants, 60cm (2ft) between rows.

HARVESTING

Spring to early autumn. Pick the shoot tips and strip off the leaves.

VARIETIES

French tarragon.

DESIGN TIPS

Pretty foliage (the plant is from the Artemisia family); looks elegant in a large pot.

COMMON PROBLEMS

Killed by cold, wet winters – offer protection.

Rust (fungal disease) – cut back the foliage. If still present on new growth, dig up the plant, wash the soil from the roots and repot in fresh compost.

↓ Cutting back the flowers of French tarragon encourages more leaves to grow.

POTS

Pot size: Minimum depth 20cm (8in); minimum diameter 20cm (8in).

Indoor windowsill: No – likes to grow tall and won't thrive in a small pot.

Produces root runners (like mint), so a bigger pot is best.

Fill containers with organic, peat-free, multipurpose potting compost.

1 plant per pot.

Keep well watered in pots, but always water in the morning, as tarragon hates having wet roots overnight.

Overfeeding spoils the flavour. Only feed monthly in summer with organic liquid/homemade feed (see page 36).

In cold areas, bring pots into a frost-free, cool place, like a porch or cold greenhouse, or raise them off the ground and cover with fleece. Do not water.

Thyme

→ Thyme flowers are beautiful, edible and attract bees.

In myth and folklore, thyme has long been associated with courage, and ladies gave their knights a sprig of thyme to bolster bravery. A powerful antiseptic in herbal medicine, thyme is another useful herb in the winter armoury (see Winter oxymel recipe, overleaf). A remarkable array of varieties is available with different forms and flowers that bees adore.

Growing tips

* Hardy perennial.
* Needs well-drained soil and a sunny position – it's a Mediterranean herb.
* A poor (less fertile) soil yields a better flavour.
* Don't overwater.
* Protect young plants with fleece in cold winters.
* Flowers are edible. Trim back after flowering to prevent the plant getting woody.

SOWING/PLANTING

For ease and quicker establishment, buy plants (see Resources, pages 220–1).

SPACINGS
(FOR POTS, SEE RIGHT)

Leave 20cm (8in) between plants, 20cm (8in) between rows.

COMMON PROBLEMS

Can die in wet conditions.

HARVESTING

Pick leaves year-round but go easy in winter.

VARIETIES

Common thyme, 'Culinary Lemon', 'Compactus', creeping white thyme, 'Jekka's Rosy Carpet', 'Elfin', 'Bressingham', 'Jekka's Red Eye'.

DESIGN TIPS

Creeping thymes look beautiful spilling over pots or between paving slabs. For success with the latter, you will need to remove part of a slab as opposed to squashing thyme into a tiny gap, as the plants need space to root.

POTS

Minimum depth: 15cm (6in); minimum diameter 15cm (6in).

Indoor windowsill: Yes.

Beautiful in hanging baskets and window boxes – plant a mix of varieties.

Fill containers with organic, peat-free, multipurpose potting compost.

Place in a sunny spot and keep containers on the dry side.

In winter, move out of the rain, if possible, or raise pots up on blocks for better drainage.

Only feed monthly in summer with organic liquid/homemade feed (see page 36).

Recipe
Winter oxymel (Fire cider)

Ingredients for 500ml (18fl oz)

½ onion, chopped

30g (1oz) fresh ginger

20g (¾oz) horseradish

20g (¾oz) fresh turmeric root, or 1 tablespoon ground turmeric

1 large (or 2 small) whole heads of garlic, cloves peeled and chopped

¼ teaspoon cayenne pepper or ½ fresh red chilli, finely chopped

2–4 tablespoons raw runny honey, plus more to taste

15–20g (½–¾oz) fresh rosemary, sage, thyme, chopped

½ lemon, sliced

Raw apple cider vinegar, to top up

From the Greek oxymeli, meaning 'acid and honey', oxymels are ancient herbal preparations made with vinegar and honey. Championed by herbalist Rosemary Gladstar, fire cider includes a mix of herbs for a supportive winter tonic. I take half a tablespoon daily, or 1 teaspoon every three hours if I have a cold. It has a potent kick, so dilute in warm water as a tea, or use in salad dressings if you find it too strong.

1 Grate the ginger, horseradish and turmeric root (if using). Place all the ingredients in a 1-litre (1¾ pint) clip-top glass jar and cover with raw apple cider vinegar.

2 Leave to infuse in a warm, dark place for 3–4 weeks. I put mine in the bottom of a kitchen cupboard.

3 Strain out the herbs using a fine-mesh strainer or muslin.

4 Sweeten with honey to taste, stirring well to dissolve. Bottle, label/date and store in the fridge. Consume within 6 months.

Note: Not suitable for children. Avoid if ou are pregnant or breastfeeding. Vinegar may aggravate acid reflux/heartburn conditions. Consult a doctor or medical herbalist if you are on medication or have underlying health conditions.

Fruit & flower spotlights

I've selected some of my favourite fruit and edible flowers that are simple to grow and viable in small spaces. You may not have bumper harvests, but I'll take a small handful of jewel-like alpine strawberries over most other fruit any day. Most of the flowers could sit happily in the herb section, but I've included them here as they are grown primarily for their flowers, not their leaves. These bursts of colour, spilling out of gaps between your vegetables, are what make edible gardening so alluring and they are essential tools in creating healthy ecosystems.

Pointers

* When buying fruit, don't just reach for the first plant you see in the garden centre. Flavour varies hugely between varieties so check out my suggestions or, in the case of apples, do some local research. You may find a heritage variety from your local area with an interesting story.
* If space is tight, you may have to be guided by small-space varieties when it comes to choosing apples and blueberries, but luckily there is still a good range of flavour options available.
* The world of marigolds can get confusing. Calendula (pot marigold) is a different plant entirely from the French marigold (*Tagetes*). French marigolds are good at repelling pests, such as whitefly, with their strong scent, while calendula is a valuable medicinal plant (see Coconut calendula salve, page 198). Both attract pollinators and beneficial insects as well as having edible flowers.

→ Tiny and sweet-tasting alpine strawberries.

Apples

→ Depending on the variety, apples are ready to harvest from August through to November.

Apples are one of the most reliable fruits you can grow in cool temperate regions. The UK had a rich heritage of apple orchards full of delightful varieties but, sadly, most have been grubbed up to make way for big agriculture or developed for housing. By planting an apple (perhaps from your local area) you can help to restore some of this history, along with the biodiversity that apple trees provide. It's also an act of giving to future generations, who will enjoy its harvests.

Growing tips

* Check rootstocks when buying apples – they dictate how big the tree will grow. M9 is a good rootstock for small gardens.
* If you only have space for one tree, check if it's self-fertile (can set fruit without cross-pollination). Otherwise you will need to grow at least one other apple from the same pollination group nearby (check with a specialist nursery).
* Trees are available as bare-root or container-grown. Bare-roots must be planted while dormant, from November to March; container-grown can be planted at any time.
* Trees need a sunny spot – avoid frost pockets.
* Water well in dry weather, especially young trees and those containers.
* With small trees, protect the spring blossom from late frost with fleece.

SOWING/PLANTING

To plant in the ground, dig a hole 3 times the diameter of the rootball (but not much deeper). Break up the sides a little with a fork and line the hole with compost or well-rotted manure. Plant the tree and hammer in a wooden tree stake carefully between the roots (saw off the stake below the bottom branches). Refill the hole with soil, firming in well. Water well and mulch with garden compost (but not right up to the stem).

Plant container-grown trees at the same depth as its potting compost – for bare-roots, look for the soil line on the stem where it was previously planted.

Staking – use a stake ⅓ the height of the tree. Place the stake on the side of the prevailing wind, which will blow the tree away from the stake and prevent any rubbing.

For planting in containers, see Pots, pages 192–3.

PRUNING

Annual pruning ensures good ventilation that wards off disease and encourages more fruit. Aim for a light summer prune from mid-July to early August and a more thorough prune in late winter. Pruning depends on the age of your tree and how it has been trained. In open ground, I find open-centred bush forms easiest to maintain.

Take a step back and assess before diving in.

Don't take more than 20 per cent of the timber out in one year.

Aim for an uncongested, open framework.

Remove the 'three Ds': anything Dead, Damaged or Diseased.

You can also buy trees as single cordons for containers, and espaliers or fans to grow against walls in small spaces – all will require slightly different pruning.

Pruning can be intimidating but it doesn't need to be. For more detailed information, see Resources, pages 220–1.

THINNING

Carefully thin clusters of fruit to 1 fruit, by cutting or twisting, to prevent them weighing down the tree and to yield larger fruit. Don't allow young trees to fruit too heavily.

SPACINGS
(FOR POTS, SEE OPPOSITE)

M26 (dwarf): Space 2.4–3.6m (8–11¾ft) apart with 4.5m (14¾ft) between rows.

M9 (dwarf): Space 2.4m (8ft) apart with 3.5m (11½ft) between rows.

HARVESTING

Trees can take 2–3 years to be productive but the flavour is worth the wait.

Do the twist test: cup an apple in your hand and twist. If ripe, it should come away without the need to pull. Different varieties ripen at different times, generally from August to October. Later varieties can be stored in a cool, frost-free place. Lay them out in boxes, without touching. Check regularly to remove any rotting fruit.

VARIETIES

Research varieties local to where you live.

Eating favourites (dessert apples): 'Ashmead's Kernel', 'Blenheim Orange', 'Cox's Orange Pippin' (susceptible to disease but the flavour is fantastic), 'Discovery', 'Egremont Russet', 'Ellison's Orange', 'Captain Kidd', 'Kidd's Orange Red', 'Lord Lambourne', 'Rosemary Russet', 'Spartan', 'Sunset', 'Worcester Pearmain'.

Cooking favourites: 'Bramley's Seedling', 'Bountiful', 'Edward VII', 'Golden Noble', 'Rev W Wilks'.

DESIGN TIPS

Underplant apples with compact nasturtiums (they can repel woolly aphids), or edge pots with chives (which reportedly reduce scab).

COMMON PROBLEMS

Commercially grown apples are often sprayed to combat pests and diseases. Organically grown apples are more susceptible to the problems below, but some resistant varieties are available (check with a nursery).

Scab – fungal patches on leaves and fruit. Generally only skin deep and doesn't affect eating. Worse in wet areas.

Coddling moth – the maggots damage fruits. Grow flowers and herbs around the trees, to attract beneficial insects.

Aphids can feed on young leaves. As for codling moth (above).

← To harvest apples, gently twist them in your hand – don't pull them from the stem.

Fill containers with two-thirds organic, peat-free, multipurpose potting compost mixed with one-third horticultural grit and a helping of garden compost or well-rotted manure.

Half-fill the pot with the compost mix; plant container-grown trees at the same depth as the potting compost they come in and bare-roots to the soil line on their stem.

Insert an upright stake carefully between the roots; firm around both with more compost. Use a tree tie to secure the stake so that it doesn't rub.

Mulch the top of the pot with rotted manure or garden compost or worm compost.

Do not allow pots to dry out – water at least twice a week, daily in hot weather.

Feed every 2 weeks from April with organic liquid/homemade feed (see page 36).

POTS

Pot size: Minimum depth 45cm (18in); minimum diameter 50cm (20in) – aim for the largest pot you can accommodate.

Select an M26 or M9 rootstock for containers. Avoid M27 – it's the smallest rootstock but becomes stressed in pots.

Use crocks (see page 37).

Blueberry

↑ For decent harvests, buy at least three blueberry plants.

A handful of blueberries for breakfast – damp with dew – taste all the sweeter from outside your door. Especially easy to grow in containers, where conditions can be controlled, they're also highly ornamental with pretty bell-like flowers and fiery autumn foliage.

Growing tips

* Requires an ericaceous (acidic) soil. Buy ericaceous potting compost for pots.
* If there's only space for 1 plant, pick a self-fertile variety, but where possible, grow 2 or more plants to improve yields through cross-pollination (check with the supplier that they flower at similar times).
* Needs a sunny, sheltered spot
* Not happy in cold, wet winters. In prolonged cold spells, raise potted plants off the ground onto bricks, move to a shed or protect the roots by insulating pots with bubble wrap.

* Use fleece to protect the flowers against late frost in spring.
* Keep well watered in summer, using rainwater if possible. Tap water is alkaline and neutralizes the acidic compost, gradually reducing yields.
* If top-dressing pots to conserve moisture, use acidic mulch: bark, leaf mould or pine needles, not compost or manure.

SOWING/PLANTING

Buy plants – see Pots, opposite, for planting.

Can be planted any time of year but aim for November to March.

In open ground, plant only if your soil pH is 5.5 or lower.

Water well, daily for the first few weeks to establish plants.

PRUNING

No need to prune in the first 2 years – just remove any congested branches.

———

From then on, prune annually in February/March, removing the 'three Ds' (anything Dead, Damaged or Diseased) and at least 1 or 2 of the oldest canes at the base, making way for new growth.

———

Cut back vigorous new shoots to a healthy bud to promote bushy plants.

SPACINGS
(FOR POTS, SEE RIGHT)

Leave 1m (39in) between plants, 1m (39in) between rows in open ground.

HARVESTING

Berries ripen gradually, turning from green to a beautiful, powdery blue.

———

For a worthwhile harvest, you'll need at least 3 plants.

———

VARIETIES

'Bluecrop' (self-fertile), 'Duke', 'North Country' (self-fertile), 'Pink Lemonade', 'Sunshine Blue' (dwarf), 'Top Hat' (dwarf).

———

DESIGN TIPS

Highly ornamental in a pot.

———

COMMON PROBLEMS

Birds – provide netting. If growing in pots, insert sticks or canes and drape the net over the top.

———

Powdery mildew – snip out the affected leaves, keep the plants mulched and well watered.

———

POTS

Pot size: Minimum depth 45cm (18in); minimum diameter 50cm (20in). These dimensions are for established plants – blueberries need potting on gradually.

When you receive your plant, pot it into the next pot size up (minimum 30cm/12in diameter) and then into a larger pot annually until you reach a nice big container.

———

Blueberries are the ideal pot plant, allowing you to grow them even without acidic soil in the garden. Just ensure you use ericaceous potting compost.

———

Fill containers with two-thirds organic, peat-free, ericaceous potting compost mixed with one-third horticultural grit.

———

Compost will then need replenishing every 2–3 years.

———

Feed monthly with an organic liquid feed (see page 36).

———

Protect pots in winter – see Growing tips, opposite.

Calendula (Pot marigold)

Brilliant orange and yellow petals unfurl with the dawn and close at sunset. Known as 'poor man's saffron', its blooms were traditionally thrown in the stew pot, giving rise to its name. It can brighten salads, stocks and baking. Calendula is one of the best first-aid kit herbs (see Recipe, page 198).

Growing tips

* Not to be confused with French marigold (*Tagetes*, see page 216).
* Enjoys a sunny position – more sun equals more flowers – but will tolerate semi-shade.
* Keep picking blooms for an ongoing supply. Pop posies in jam jars to brighten your home.
* Easy to save the seeds – wait for the flower heads to turn brown at the end of the season. Will likely self-set around your garden.

SOWING/PLANTING

Sow in August/September or from March to May.

August/September sowings will yield earlier flowers the following spring. Sow indoors in modules. Cover the seed with compost. Thin to 1 seedling per module. Overwinter in an unheated greenhouse or cold frame. Pot on if necessary and plant out from April.

Alternatively, direct sow outdoors in beds or pots in August or September, thinning in spring (see Spacings, below).

Alternatively, sow from March to May in modules or direct sow outside.

Cover outdoor seedlings with fleece in winter cold snaps, and protect early sowings/plantings in spring.

SPACINGS
(FOR POTS, SEE OPPOSITE)

Leave 20cm (8in) between plants, 30cm (12in) between rows.

HARVESTING

Culinary – use petals fresh or dry the flower heads, separating off the petals for winter stews.

Medicinal use – pick flowers when half-open on a dry morning; keep the green resinous base attached, as most of the medicinal oils are found here. Allow any insects to escape; use a herb drying rack or spread out on trays indoors with good airflow. Store in airtight jars in a cool, dark place once dry.

VARIETIES

Calendula officinalis (orange and yellow varieties), 'Indian Prince', 'Flashback Mix'.

DESIGN TIPS

Use to line paths and bed ends; dot pots of calendula between vegetable containers – they're a magnet for pollinators and beneficial insects.

→ Calendula flowers are edible, medicinal and look beautiful in a vase.

COMMON PROBLEMS

Slugs (see page 79) and aphids (see page 80) can cause problems.

Powdery mildew (see page 84) – strikes later in the season. If affected, cut the whole plant back to 20cm (8in) above ground and await new growth. Keep moist.

POTS

Pot size: Minimum depth 15cm (6in); minimum diameter 15cm (6in), bigger is better.

Indoor windowsill: Yes – although vulnerable to whitefly.

Beautiful in pots and window boxes.

Fill containers with organic, peat-free, multipurpose potting compost.

Stand in a sunny spot, keep well watered and feed with organic liquid/homemade feed every 2 weeks (see page 36).

Recipe
Coconut calendula salve

Ingredients for approximately 275ml (9fl oz) infused oil. (You will need 240ml (8fl oz) for the salve, so you may have a little left over for other projects.)

400ml (13½fl oz) coconut oil

30g dried calendula flowers (use any *Calendula officinalis* varieties but orange and yellow types are most common medicinally)

Note: DO NOT let any moisture get into the oil, as it will spoil. Ensure all the equipment is dry and that you wipe the bottom of the bowl with a tea towel before pouring into the jug. Use dried calendula flowers, not fresh, for the same reason.

A soothing salve for tired gardener's hands or skin irritations – think stings, burns, eczema, scrapes and grazes.

1 Place the coconut oil in a bain-marie (a heatproof bowl over a saucepan part-filled with simmering water). Allow the coconut oil to melt.

2 Add the flowers and leave to infuse for 3 hours over a gentle simmer – do not cover and do not allow the water in the pan to dry out.

3 For a stronger infusion, strain after 2–3 hours and repeat the process with the same oil and a fresh batch of flowers.

4 Remove from the heat. Line a sieve or funnel with muslin and strain the oil into a clean jug. When cool enough, squeeze out as much oil as possible from the muslin. The discarded flowers can go for composting.

5 You can use this oil directly on the skin, but I like to make it into a salve, as it's less messy.

Ingredients for approximately 240ml (8fl oz) salve

240ml (9fl oz) coconut calendula-infused oil (see opposite)

35g (1¼oz) beeswax pellets

20 drops of lavender essential oil (optional)

Dried calendula petals to decorate (optional)

You will also need 20 × 15ml (½fl oz) lip balm tins or 4 × 60ml (2fl oz) jars (see Resources for equipment supplies, pages 220–1)

1 If using glass jars, make sure to sterilize them (see page 159).

2 Lay out all your tins or jars and remove the lids before you start. Beeswax starts to set once removed from the heat, so you need to move swiftly.

3 Heat the calendula oil and beeswax over a bain-marie (see method opposite) until the beeswax is melted. Whisk with a fork to speed up the process.

4 Remove from the heat and mix in the essential oil, if using. Now you need to move fast as the wax will start to set. Using oven gloves, carefully pour the mixture into a jug, taking care to avoid any water drips falling into it.

5 From the jug, pour into tins or jars of your choosing.

6 Decorate with dried calendula petals if you wish.

7 Allow the salve to set, pop on the lids, label/date. Use within 6 months. The salve hardens in cold weather, but can be quickly softened in your hands.

Nasturtium

More than just a lure for pollinators and beneficial insects, nasturtiums are an edible flower with genuine kitchen credentials. Salads, butters and pickles all benefit from the flowers, leaves and seed pods of this peppery plant (see Recipes, overleaf).

Growing tips

* One of the easiest flowers to grow. Enjoys a sunny spot.
* Likes a well-drained, poor soil for maximum flowering. Will romp away in fertile soil, but puts on more leaf and fewer flowers. (See Pots, below.)
* For the same reason, don't overwater – a few times a week should suffice.
* Deadhead for prolonged flowering.
* Flowers into the autumn, but killed by the first frosts.
* Use to lure blackfly away from your vegetables.

SOWING/PLANTING

Sow from April to June.

Sow indoors in modules or small pots in April. Cover the seed with compost.

Thin to 1 seedling per module/pot.

Plant out once all danger of frost has passed from mid- to late May.

Alternatively, direct sow into beds or pots from mid-late May to June. Simply pop the large seeds in with your fingers, to 2cm (¾in) deep, where you want the plants to grow. Sow a few seeds per station, thinning to 1.

SPACINGS
(FOR POTS, SEE OPPOSITE)

Leave 20cm (8in) between plants, 20cm (8in) between rows.

HARVESTING

Pick flowers and leaves fresh to use in salads.

Seeds should be picked just before their green colour fades.

VARIETIES

'Tall Mix', 'Trailing Mixed', 'Empress of India' (climbing/ trailing), 'Alaska'. 'Black Velvet' (compact) is best for mixed containers, as other varieties may take over.

DESIGN TIPS

Plant at bed edges to lure in pollinators, or interplant with squashes or kale.

Trailing/climbing varieties can be trained up supports.

COMMON PROBLEMS

Cabbage white butterfly – caterpillars eat the leaves (see page 80). Pick off by hand or accept the plant as a sacrificial crop, deterring them from your brassicas.

Blackfly infest stems and undersides of leaves. Treat as a sacrificial crop or see Aphids, page 80, for solutions.

→ Nasturtiums make perfect pot companions, spilling prettily over the edges.

POTS

Pot size: Minimum depth 20cm (8in); minimum diameter 20cm (8in).

Great in pots, window boxes and hanging baskets. Plant at the edges, allowing them to spill over.

Indoor windowsill: Yes, but only as microgreens – pick the leaves when small.

Fill containers with organic, peat-free, multipurpose potting compost, or if you have a pot containing last season's compost, use this as it will yield more flowers.

Do not plant more than 1 per pot, especially with other vegetables, as it will take over.

Stand in a sunny spot, water only once or twice a week, and don't feed the pots.

Recipe
Nasturtium butter

Once picked, allow any insects to escape the flowers by leaving them on a tray near an open window, or outside in the shade.

**Ingredients
for 250g (9oz)**

40 nasturtium flowers chopped (will work with less)

250g (9oz) butter at room temperature

1 garlic clove, crushed

½ tablespoon lemon juice

Salt and pepper

A colourful way to preserve the peppery flowers. I often use a recipe from the legendary Alice Waters' Chez Panisse pasta book: sauté sliced baby courgettes and shallots in nasturtium butter with parsley and thyme, simmer in a little vegetable stock, then stir through pasta with more butter. It's a beautiful dish. Nasturtium butter is also delicious baked with fish.

1 Mix all the ingredients in a bowl and season to taste with salt and pepper.

2 Spoon out on to a sheet of parchment paper and roll tightly into a log. Twist at both ends. There is a knack to achieving a taut roll! There are plenty of online videos that will show you how to do this.

3 Place in the fridge to firm up.

4 Rounds can be sliced off with a warm knife as needed – use within 5 days. Alternatively, freeze for up to 6 months (cut into sections and freeze separately).

Recipe
Pickled nasturtium seeds (Poor man's capers)

Ingredients for 1 × 250g (9oz) jar

100g (3½oz) nasturtium seeds (green)

15g (3 teaspoons) salt

200ml (7fl oz) white wine vinegar

3–4 peppercorns, slightly crushed

A few herb sprigs (optional) – try tarragon, thyme or bay

You will also need a 250g (9oz) jar

If you're a caper fiend, this recipe is a thriftier route to the same tangy treat, adapted here from Preserves: River Cottage Handbook No.2 *by Pam Corbin. Pick the seeds just before their green colour fades – once brown, they are past their best.*

1 Place the seeds in a bowl and cover with 300ml (10fl oz) water. Add the salt and stir to dissolve.

2 Cover the bowl with a clean tea towel and leave the seeds to sit in the brine for 24 hours. There will be a mild sulphur-like smell, which is part of the pickling process!

3 Drain and rinse the seeds. Lay the seeds on trays lined with kitchen paper to dry. Meanwhile, sterilize your jar (see page 159).

4 Once dry, place the seeds in the sterilized jar(s) with the pappercorns and herbs and cover completely with the vinegar.

5 Seal with a lid (if using a metal lid, place a layer of parchment paper between the top of the jar and lid, as vinegar erodes metal).

6 Store in a cool, dark place. They will be ready to eat after 2 weeks. Once opened, store in the fridge, keeping submerged in vinegar.

Rhubarb

Well suited to the UK climate, rhubarb was coveted by the Victorians, who used it in everything from jams and jellies to pies and fools. This tradition is still upheld in the 'rhubarb triangle' of West Yorkshire, where 90 per cent of the world's rhubarb was once grown. This fuss-free vegetable (rhubarb is actually a vegetable, not a fruit) returns every year with plentiful harvests.

Growing tips

* Perennial.
* Needs a sunny spot and deep, fertile soil.
* Likes well-drained, moist (not waterlogged) soil. Don't let it dry out.
* Foliage dies back in winter.
* Vigorous plants need a large container or their own area in the garden.
* Remove flowering stalks.
* Divide plants after 4 years to make new stock.

SOWING/PLANTING

For quicker establishment, buy young crowns from a nursery or pinch a piece of root from a friend's established plant. These need planting from October to February, with the growing point at soil level.

Pot-grown plants are also available and can be planted at any time, but spring and autumn are best.

Add well-rotted manure or compost to the soil or pots before planting.

Mulch with compost or well-rotted manure in spring.

FORCING

For extra early harvests, rhubarb can be forced. This produces sweet, tender, hot-pink stems that many consider superior in flavour. There's a place for both.

Choose early varieties to force (see Varieties, page 206).

1 Place a tall pot or dustbin over crowns in January. Insulate the base of the upturned pot with manure or compost. Place a brick on top to weigh it down. If you can source a terracotta 'rhubarb forcer', you're in luck. The lack of light blanches the stems, turning them pink.

2 Check the stems regularly – they'll be ready for picking within 6–8 weeks.

3 Once you've picked the forced stems, remove the forcer and don't pick from this plant for the rest of the season – it needs to replenish. And don't force the same plant year on year.

Forcing rhubarb in a pot may put the plant under unnecessary stress. I'd stick to cropping pot-grown plants a little later in the year.

→ The vibrant pink stems of forced early rhubarb.

→ Rhubarb 'Fulton's Strawberry Surprise', a mid-season variety.

SPACINGS
(FOR POTS, SEE RIGHT)

Leave 1m (39in) between plants, 1m (39in) between rows.

HARVESTING

1–2 plants will be ample for 2 people over the season.

Don't harvest plants in the first year after planting – they need to build up a good root system. Pick lightly in the second year. By the third year you can harvest until midsummer.

Grip the stems at the base, push down, twist and pull. Do not cut, as this leads to rotting. When cropping, always leave half the stems intact. Stop cropping in July. Plants need the remaining leaves to store energy for the following season.

The leaves are not edible – cut them off and compost.

VARIETIES

Early: 'Timperley Early', 'Champagne'.

Mid-season: 'Victoria', 'Fulton's Strawberry Surprise', 'Collis Ruby'.

DESIGN TIPS

This large-leaved handsome plant makes a statement in a large container.

COMMON PROBLEMS

Largely problem-free.

Slugs like lurking in containers and forcing pots, so keep an eye out and remove them.

POTS

Pot size: Minimum depth 60cm (2ft); minimum diameter 60cm (2ft) – the bigger, the better. A half-barrel or a wide-topped dustbin, with holes drilled for drainage, works well.

Fill containers with organic, peat-free, multipurpose potting compost, enriched with plenty of well-rotted manure or garden compost.

Do not plant more than 1 plant per pot.

Stand in a sunny spot, keep well watered and feed with organic liquid or homemade feed every 2 weeks (see page 36).

Recipe
Rhubarb shrub

Ingredients for 1 litre (1¾ pints)

700g (1lb 9oz) red or pink rhubarb cut into 3cm (1in) slices

40g (1½oz) fresh ginger, peeled and grated

300g (10½oz) caster or unrefined sugar

500ml (18fl oz) water

400ml (14fl oz) raw apple cider vinegar

Sparkling water

You will also need a 1 litre (1¾ pint) glass bottle, sterilized (see page 159)

Shrubs, aka drinking vinegars, are ancient drinks, made by mixing fruit, herbs, vinegar and sugar. You're left with a zingy sweet/sour syrup to mix with sparkling water (like a cordial) or add to cocktails. A range of fruit and herbs can be used, but I especially love a rhubarb shrub for its extra tang – it's very addictive.

1 Place the rhubarb, ginger, sugar and water in a pan and bring to the boil over a medium heat. Turn the heat down and simmer until the rhubarb disintegrates (usually 10–15 minutes).

2 Strain the rhubarb syrup through a muslin-lined sieve into a non-metallic jug or bowl. Ensure you press out all the juice with a spatula. (Eat the discarded rhubarb with yogurt or porridge.)

3 Once the syrup has cooled, add the vinegar. It should have a tangy punch.

4 Pour into the sterilized bottle and store in the fridge.

5 Serve over ice with sparkling water, as you would a cordial. Or add a glug of gin. Consume within 2 weeks.

Rose geranium
(Scented pelargonium)

Perhaps the sweetest smelling of all the herbs, rose geranium is best grown where you can easily brush against it. Celebrated for its essential oil used in cosmetics, the leaves and edible flowers can also be used in a range of culinary treats. Infuse leaves into stewed fruit, jams, vinegars, syrups, teas, cream, baking and desserts. (See Rose geranium syrup, page 211.)

← Rose geranium 'Attar of Roses', with its scented leaves and delicate pink flowers.

Growing tips

* Tender perennial.
* Pretty lobed foliage and soft pink edible flowers.
* Originally from South Africa, so enjoys a sunny, sheltered spot with well-drained soil.
* Killed by frost. Plant out after the last frost in May. See also Overwintering, page 210.
* Not thirsty plants, so don't overwater.
* Younger plants tend to be more productive, so keep rejuvenating your stock with cuttings.
* If grown in warm, dry, light conditions, like a windowsill, plants will provide foliage and flowers year-round.
* Replenish compost in pots every year.

CUTTINGS

Buy young plants or take cuttings from existing plants, which is very easy to do. Cuttings taken in late summer will need to be overwintered on a warm windowsill or in a heated greenhouse.

1 Cut a stem with a sharp knife just above a leaf node (little raised lines where the leaves emerge) on the parent plant.

2 Strip the lower leaves, leaving just the top pair. Pinch out any potential flowering shoots.

3 Short cuttings are best, so trim each stem to 8cm (3in), cutting just below a leaf node.

4 Fill 8–9cm (3–3½in) pots with multipurpose compost, adding a little grit if you have some but it's not essential.

5 Push 3 cuttings per pot into the compost, to 2–3cm (¾–1in) deep, around the edge of each pot. Water the compost.

6 Stand in a light, dry place, warm for overwintering cuttings, cool for summer cuttings. Keep the compost moist. A good root system will occur within 6–8 weeks.

7 For overwintered cuttings, repot into individual pots in March/April and plant out once any sign of frost has passed. Spring-grown cuttings can be potted on and set out after the last frost.

SPACINGS
(FOR POTS, SEE PAGE 210)

Leave 45cm (18in) between plants, 45cm (18in) between rows.

HARVESTING

Pick individual leaves and flowers as needed.

← Rub the leaves to release the sweet scent of roses.

Overwintering

Before the first frosts, either give plants in pots a light trim and bring inside to a windowsill/conservatory, where they will keep growing, or cut back by two-thirds and move to a cool greenhouse or cold frame and cover with fleece. Water the latter plants sparingly, keeping them on the dry side until they reshoot in spring. Provide a little heat or extra insulation on the coldest nights. As insurance, use the growth you have removed to take cuttings. This can also be done in spring/summer (see page 209). If plants are in the ground, lift before the first frost and pot up, following either of the steps above.

VARIETIES

'Attar of Roses'.

DESIGN TIPS

Beautiful foliage spills over the front of borders and pots.

COMMON PROBLEMS

Pelargonium rust – starts as small yellow spots on the leaves. Keep plants well ventilated and replace if severe infection takes hold.

POTS

Pot size: Minimum depth 20cm (8in); minimum diameter 20cm (8in).

Indoor windowsill: Yes – cuttings/young plants will grow in 1-litre (1¾ pint) pots 11cm (4in) deep and 13cm (5in) in diameter.

As always, the bigger the pot, the more productive it will be – 3 plants in a large pot creates a lovely display. Plants also work well in hanging baskets.

Fill containers with organic, peat-free, multipurpose potting compost.

Stand in a sunny spot, water moderately and feed with organic liquid/homemade feed every 2 weeks (see page 36).

Recipe
Rose geranium syrup

Ingredients

5–10 rose geranium leaves

1 cupful of water

1 cupful of sugar

Juice of ½ lemon

You will also need a 500ml (17fl oz) glass jar/bottle, sterilized (see page 159)

Delicious with gin, vodka or drizzled over ice cream with summer berries, or use it to sweeten your Lemon Verbena Iced Tea (see page 171). Rosemary, mint and lemon verbena also make wonderful syrups.

1 Put the rose geranium leaves in a pan with the water and sugar over a low heat. Stir to dissolve the sugar, then increase the heat and boil for 5 minutes.

2 Remove from the heat, add the lemon juice and allow to cool.

3 Strain and bottle. Will keep in the fridge for 1 week.

Strawberries

→ Alpine strawberries, the ultimate garden snack.

It is easy to see why strawberries picked in their rightful season, fresh from the plant, are universally loved. And there are few things more disappointing than watery, out-of-season, supermarket strawberries. To experience the real magic, it's imperative to grow your own. Even in a tiny space, a pot of alpine strawberries will bring you tiny pops of intense flavour. I first grew alpine strawberries at Le Manoir aux Quat'Saisons, in a shady border at the top of the vegetable garden. I often made a diversion here on my way to the kitchen, to gobble a few – I'm sure I wasn't the only one; they really are the queen of all garden snacks.

Growing tips

* Hardy perennial.
* Ensure the ground is well manured or composted in advance of planting.
* Likes a sunny spot, but tolerates a little shade.
* Keep well-watered, as plants dry out fast.
* Mulch with well-rotted manure or compost to conserve moisture.
* Protect flowers from late spring frosts using fleece.
* Remove runners (horizontal stems that root in nearby soil and produce more plants), as they deplete the parent plant, unless you want new plants (see Runners, page 214).
* Replace plants every 3 years for best yields. Replant in a different bed or if in pots, use fresh compost.
* Tidy plants after fruiting. Cut back to new leaves, 10cm (4in) above the crown, to promote new growth. Perpetual varieties don't need cutting back; just remove the older leaves in autumn.

SOWING/PLANTING

Source quality plants or take runners from established plants (see Runners, page 214).

Buy early, mid-season or late-season plants that fruit in succession from early June into July. Perpetual varieties, or everbearers, yield small flushes in short bursts across the season into autumn.

Strawberry plants can be purchased as pot-grown plants, bare-rooted runners or cold-stored runners.

Pot-grown: Plant at any time but avoid December/January – plants provide good crops after planting.

Bare-rooted runners: Bundles of runners (see Runners, page 214) sold ready for immediate planting in autumn or spring. More economical than pot-grown but they don't crop heavily in the first year.

Cold-stored runners: Runners for planting from April to June that crop well that season. Good for impatient gardeners.

The best planting time is August/September for crops the following year. Plantings in October and March/April are also possible but will not yield big harvests in the first season.

Make a hole that accommodates the roots. Ensure the crown (knobbly cluster above the roots) is planted level with the soil surface; if it's below the surface, it can rot; if too high, it can dry out. Firm in well and water.

RUNNERS

Plants produce runners (stems that root), from which you can easily make new plants. Allow them to root firmly in the ground next to the plant, then cut the stem linking the runner to the parent plant and pot into small individual pots to grow on. If you're growing the parent strawberry in a pot, place runners in small pots (around the parent plant) and peg down to keep in contact with the soil. Snip the stem when rooted.

SPACINGS
(FOR POTS, SEE OPPOSITE)

Leave 45cm (18in) between plants, 75cm (30in) between rows.

Alpines: 30cm (12in) between plants, 30cm (12in) between rows.

HARVESTING

Grow at least 5 plants for decent yields of berries.

Pick when they're bright red, warmed by the sun; pick white varieties of alpine strawberries when plump and delightfully sweet.

Remove mouldy fruit.

VARIETIES

Early season: 'Gariguette', 'Malling Centenary', 'Marshmello', 'Royal Sovereign', 'Sweetheart'.

Mid-season: 'Cambridge Favourite'.

Late season: 'Florence', 'Malwina'.

Perpetual: 'Mara des Bois', 'Malling Opal'.

Alpine: 'Mignonette', 'White Soul', 'Alexandria'.

DESIGN TIPS

Alpine strawberries make a
lovely edible edge to borders,
pots or under fruit trees.

———

COMMON PROBLEMS

Birds – use netting for
protection, or like me, share
your alpine strawberries with
the birds; there are enough
to go round.

———

Slugs (see page 79).

———

If plants look sickly, stunted and
do not recover, they may have
a virus – remove plants (do not
compost) and start again in
different soil.

———

Grey Mould – fungal growth
affecting plant and fruit in
damp, humid conditions.
Cut out and remove the
infected areas.

———

POTS

Pot size: Minimum depth
20cm (8in); minimum diameter
20cm (8in).

———

Indoor windowsill: Yes – alpine
strawberries in a 2-litre (3½ pint)
pot 13cm (5in) deep and 17cm
(6½in) in diameter.

———

Pots, hanging baskets, grow
bags and window boxes all work
well. Avoid traditional terracotta
strawberry planter pots – they
look pretty but dry out too fast.

———

Aim for 4 plants to a 35cm (14in)
diameter pot or hanging basket,
or 5 to a grow bag.

———

Fill containers with organic,
peat-free, multipurpose potting
compost, top-dressing with
worm compost or garden
compost or well-rotted manure
to retain moisture.

———

Stand in a sunny spot, keep well
watered and feed with organic
liquid/homemade feed every
2 weeks while flowering and
fruiting (see page 36).

———

Alpine strawberries

———

Sow from seed indoors in
February. Sow into seed
trays on the soil surface,
lightly cover and pop
inside a clear plastic bag to
raise humidity. The seeds
need a temperature of
18–21°C (64–71°F) degrees
to germinate, which may
take time. When large
enough to handle, prick
out, pot on and plant out in
May. Follow Growing tips,
page 212, although not all
alpine varieties produce
runners. Many reproduce
themselves by setting seed.

French marigolds

↑ Mahogany-flowered *Tagetes linnaeus.*

A traditional companion for tomatoes, the foliage emits a pungent smell that can repel whitefly – it has always worked for me. Fiery shades of orange, yellow and mahogany petals look striking as cut flowers or scattered through salads and desserts for a citrus zing.

Growing tips

* Half-hardy annual. Plant out after threat of frost has passed.
* Likes full sun in a sheltered spot. Keep well watered.
* Interplant tomatoes and other greenhouse crops. Tuck into outside pots to attract pollinators.
* Regular deadheading will keep the blooms coming. Continues flowering until killed by the first frosts.
* Collect seed from dried seedheads in late summer, to use the following year.

SOWING/PLANTING

Sow from March to May indoors in modules. Cover the seed with compost.

Thin to 1 per module once germinated.

Pot on if necessary, to 9cm (3½in) pots, and plant out in May after the last frosts.

Alternatively, direct sow into beds/pots from mid- to late May, protecting seedlings with fleece. Thin to the spacings below.

SPACINGS
(FOR POTS, SEE RIGHT)

Leave 30cm (12in) between plants in beds, or 15cm (6in) between plants in pots for a full display.

COMMON PROBLEMS

Trouble-free.

HARVESTING

Edible flowers – separate the petals.

VARIETIES

French marigolds (Tagetes *patula*): 'Nana', 'Burning Embers', 'Strawberry Blond'.

Other Tagetes (not French but still pretty): *T. tenuifolia, T. linnaeus.*

POTS

Pot size: Minimum depth 15cm (6in); minimum diameter 15cm (6in), bigger is better.

Indoor windowsills: No – does not thrive.

Fill containers with organic, peat-free, multipurpose compost 3 plants to a 30cm (12in) pot. Stand in a sunny spot, keep well watered and feed with organic liquid/homemade feed every 2 weeks (see page 36).

Viola

By far the prettiest edible flower, dainty violas with their merry nodding heads bring cheer to salads, drinks and desserts, and they're long associated with healing broken hearts.

Growing tips

✳ Grow as a hardy annual.
✳ Flowers in spring/summer and winter.
✳ Grow in sun or partial shade.
✳ Keep picking for continuous blooms.
✳ Don't overwater in winter.

SOWING/PLANTING

For spring/summer flowering, sow indoors in modules in March or September (September yields earlier blooms).

Overwinter autumn sowings in a cold frame or cold greenhouse, hardening off and planting out the following spring.

Violas need complete darkness to germinate so cover seed completely with compost.

Thin to 1 seedling per module.

For winter flowering, sow in modules from June to July for autumn planting.

SPACINGS
(FOR POTS, SEE RIGHT)

15cm (6in) between plants, 15cm (6in) between rows.

HARVESTING

Pick flowers when fully open.

VARIETIES

There are many varieties, all edible, but traditional Viola tricolor 'Heartsease' is my favourite.

DESIGN TIPS

Violas make beautiful edging around pots of taller vegetables or in hanging baskets.

COMMON PROBLEMS

Trouble-free.

↑ Viola tricolor 'Heartsease' and calendula in ice cubes. Fill each mould halfway with water. Add the flowers and top up before freezing.

POTS

Pot size: Minimum depth 10cm (4in); minimum diameter 10cm (4in).

Indoor windowsill: Yes.

Violas look pretty grouped in small terracotta pots. But the smaller the pot, the quicker it will dry out, so plants will need daily watering.

Fill containers with organic, peat-free, multipurpose potting compost.

Shade from the midday sun if on a south-facing windowsill, or grow on an east- or west-facing sill.

Outside, keep well watered and feed with organic liquid/homemade feed every 2 weeks (see page 36).

The jargon

Annual
A plant that completes its life cycle in one year.

Bare-root
Plant arrives with no soil around roots (not in a pot). A cheaper way of sending plants when they are dormant.

Biennial
A plant that completes its life cycle in two years.

Bolting
A plant stressed by its conditions or grown at the wrong time of year will flower and produce seed. It knows it is on its way out and is trying to reproduce quickly.

Brassica
Plants in the cabbage/mustard family. My Top 30 brassicas include kale, radish, rocket, mustard, Asian greens and land cress.

Crocks
Broken pieces of terracotta, placed over drainage holes in pots, to aid drainage.

Cut-and-come-again
Usually leafy vegetables that regrow after each cut, or harvest.

Deadheading
Removal of dead flowers to keep the plant productive and tidy.

Direct sowing
Sowing seed direct into the soil as opposed to raising seedlings in pots or modules first.

Drill
Shallow furrow made in the soil to sow seeds into.

Frost hardy
Plants that can withstand frost and cold temperatures.

Frost tender
Plants that will not survive frost.

Garden compost
Usually homemade with decomposed vegetable kitchen scraps, leaves, garden waste, cardboard and sometimes animal manures. Adds nutrients to the soil.

Germination
When a seed breaks dormancy and shoots.

Half-hardy
Plants killed by freezing temperatures.

Hardening off
Acclimatizing plants grown indoors to cooler conditions outside, by moving them outside for incresingly longer periods each day.

Hardy
Plants that can withstand low temperatures.

Leggy
If plants lack light, stems become abnormally long and floppy (often accelerated by warm conditions) and the plant can't support itself.

Mulch
A layer of material (either organic, like compost, or inorganic, like plastic) that covers the soil surface. Can reduce weeds, hold moisture, add nutrients, warm the ground or protect plant roots from cold.

Perennial
A plant that lives for more than two years.

Pinching out
The removal of the growing tip of the plant or its sideshoots, to encourage growth in the remainder of the plant.

Pollination
Pollen is transferred within or between plants, either naturally by wind, birds and insect life or by humans. Leads to the production of seeds and the next generation of the plant.

Potting on
Moving young plants into larger pots to enable them to grow on with additional space and nutrients.

Propagate
Making new plants by sowing seeds, taking cuttings and dividing plants.

Rootbound
If a plant becomes too big for its pot, the roots will often wrap around the inside of the pot, weakening the plant.

Seed leaves
The first set of leaves that a seedling produces.

Seedling
A little plant either with its seed leaves or true leaves.

Self-seeding/self-set
When a plant disperses its seeds naturally itself.

Station sowing
Sowing seed in situ where you wish the plant to be. This saves time spent thinning plants.

Top-dressing
Applying mulch on beds/pots to add nutrients and conserve water, or for decorative effect.

Top soil
The very top layer of soil that holds most of the nutrients and organic matter for growing.

True leaves
The second set of leaves that a seedling produces.

Variety
A form of a particular species. For example, if the species is beetroot (*Beta vulgaris*), the variety is 'Detroit' or 'Golden'. Often used interchangeably with 'cultivar'.

Weed
An (often wild) plant that has popped up somewhere where it is not wanted. Weeds are often vilified but can be useful (see page 86).

MONTH	SEASON
January	Mid-winter
February	Late Winter
March	Early Spring
April	Mid-spring
May	Late Spring
June	Early Summer
July	Mid-summer
August	Late Summer
September	Early Autumn
October	Mid-autumn
November	Late Autumn
December	Early Winter

Resources

SEED SUPPLIERS

Real Seeds
realseeds.co.uk

Seed Co-operative
seedcooperative.org.uk

Vital Seeds
vitalseeds.co.uk

The Organic
Gardening Catalogue
organiccatalogue.com

Cotswold Grass Seeds
(for green manure)
cotswoldseeds.com

SkySprouts Organics
(for bulk microgreen
seed)
skysprouts.co.uk

Adaptive Seeds (US)
adaptiveseeds.com

High Mowing (US)
highmowingseeds.com

Johnny's (US)
johnnyseeds.com

Territorial Seed
Company (US)
territorialseed.com

ORGANIC VEGETABLE PLANTS

Organic Plants
organicplants.co.uk

Rocket Gardens
rocketgardens.co.uk

HERB NURSERIES

The Cottage Herbery
thecottageherbery.co.uk

Jekka's
jekkas.com

Herbal Haven
herbalhaven.com

Norfolk Herbs
norfolkherbs.co.uk

Poyntzfield Herb
Nursery
poyntzfieldherbs.co.uk

FRUIT NURSERIES

Brandy Carr Nurseries
(for rhubarb)
brandycarrnurseries.co.uk

Otter Farm
otterfarm.co.uk

Walcot Organic
Nursery
walcotnursery.co.uk

Trees of Antiquity (US)
treesofantiquity.com

GARDENING EQUIPMENT

Gardening-Naturally
(for module trays and
more)
gardening-naturally.com

Containerwise
Materials Handling
(for module trays)
containerwise.co.uk

Plastic Free Gardening
plasticfreegardening.com

Johnny's (US)
johnnyseeds.com

Territorial Seed
Company (US)
territorialseed.com

Salvage yards are also
a valuable resource for
recycled containers and
plant supports

TOOLS

Implementations
implementations.co.uk

Sneeboer
sneeboer.co.uk

ORGANIC PEAT-FREE SEED & POTTING COMPOST

This list is not
exhaustive, but I have
had success with all
these:

Carbon Gold
carbongold.com

Dalefoot Composts
(Long lasting nutrients)
dalefootcomposts.co.uk

Fertile Fibre
fertilefibre.com

Melcourt
melcourt.co.uk

Bio365 (US)
www.bio365.com

BULK COMPOST

Always look locally first.

Compost Direct
compostdirect.com

Material Change
material-change.com

Mr Muck
mrmuck.co.uk

WORM COMPOSTING

Wiggly Wigglers
wigglywigglers.co.uk

The Urban Worm
theurbanworm.co.uk

PLANT FEED

Maxicrop Seaweed Feed (widely available)

Natural Grower
naturalgrower.co.uk

Remin Volcanic Rock Dust
reminscotland.com

SEED SAVING

Garden Organic's Heritage Seed Library
gardenorganic.org.uk

Real Seeds
realseeds.co.uk

Seed Sovereignty (a huge range of resources)
seedsovereignty.info

Vital Seeds
vitalseeds.co.uk

Native Seeds/SEARCH (US) *nativeseeds.org*

Seed Savers Exchange (US) *seedsavers.org*

FRUIT TREE PRUNING

Natural England (for advice on traditional orchards, maintenance and pruning)
naturalengland.org.uk/publication/25004

RHS
rhs.org.uk

DRIED HERBS & EQUIPMENT FOR REMEDY MAKING

G. Baldwin & Co
baldwins.co.uk

Organic Herb Trading (for bulk orders)
organicherbtrading.com

Star Child
starchild.co.uk

Hackney Herbal (for herbal resources and workshops)
hackneyherbal.com

FURTHER READING

A Taste of the Unexpected by Mark Diacono

Back Garden Seed Saving by Sue Stickland

Forage by Liz Knight

Fruit Trees for Every Garden by Orin Martin & Manjula Martin

Hedgerow Medicine by Julie Bruton-Seal and Matthew Seal

How to Prune an Apple Tree by Chloe Ward

Jekka's Complete Herb Book by Jekka McVicar

Organic Gardening: The Natural No-Dig Way by Charles Dowding

The Organic Salad Garden by Joy Larkom & Roger Phillips

PODCASTS

farmerama.co

USEFUL WEBSITES

charlesdowding.co.uk

farmstofeedus.org

gardenorganic.co.uk

landinournames.community

sustainablefoodtrust.org

Index

Bold pagination = main entry; *italic* = illustrations

Acknowledgements

This book was commissioned when my daughter was only six-months old, so to Hugo, Mum and Dad – thank you for the hours and days you gave up to make this happen. Writing a book is a breeze in comparison to childcare!

To my wise, encouraging teachers who ignited these green fingers – my grandmother Daphne, Robert and Gill Hocking, Sean O'Neill, Orin Martin, Scott Kleinrock, Nicola Bradley, Raymond Blanc and Charles Dowding. To Jamie Oliver and the Fifteen Cornwall team – Andy Appleton and Polly Dent who supported me from the start.

To Nick Jones for a blank canvas and many grey hairs. To all my garden team mates who I have worked alongside over the years.

To Jason Ingram for his pictures and making every shoot day such fun. To Alice Maccoll for her lovely illustrations. To Alison Starling, Sybella Stephens and Jonathan Christie for guiding me through my first book so graciously. To Francesca Zampi and Found for believing in me. To Emma Dalton, Maya Thomas and Lisa Pedley for culinary and herbal wisdom. To Ben Raskin for his 'organic' expertise. To Aradia Crockett for sprucing me up. To Zoe Hitchner and Ian Wilson for advice from across the pond. And to Bonnie, the best thing I've ever grown.